C000262340

Healing the Human Spirit

Deeper Healing for the Human Spirit

Combined edition

Ruth Hawkey

New Wine Press

New Wine Press
PO Box 17
Chichester
West Sussex
PO19 2AW
England

Copyright © 1996, 2004 Ruth Hawkey

This combined edition was formerly published as two separate
titles, now only available separately as print on demand. Please
contact the publisher for further details.

All rights reserved. No part of this publication may be
reproduced, stored in a retrieval system, or transmitted, in any
form or by any means, electronic, mechanical, photocopying,
recording or otherwise, without the prior permission of the
publisher.

Short extracts may be used for review purposes.

Scripture quotations in *Healing the Human Spirit* are taken from
The Amplified Bible. Old Testament copyright © 1965, 1987 by
the Zondervan Corporation. The Amplified New Testament
copyright © 1958, 1987 by the Lockman Foundation. Used by
permission.

Scripture quotations in *Deeper Healing for the Human Spirit* are
taken from the New King James Version, copyright 1983 by
Thomas Nelson, Inc.

ISBN: 978 1 905991 41 9

Typeset by CRB Associates, Potterhanworth, Lincolnshire
Printed in Malta

Healing the Human Spirit

Contents

Preface

According to the Scriptures man is a tripartite being, which means that he has been created with three parts to his nature: body, soul and spirit. Saint Paul writing to the church at Thessalonica says:

> *'May the God who gives us peace make you holy in every way and keep your whole being – spirit, soul, and body – free from every fault at the coming of our Lord Jesus Christ.'*
>
> (1 Thessalonians 5:23)

and the writer to the Hebrews confirms the three-fold nature of man:

> *'The word of God is alive and active, sharper than any double-edged sword. It cuts all the way through, to where soul and spirit meet, to where joints and marrow come together.'*
>
> (Hebrews 4:12)

However, whilst there are a number of books

7

available concerned with the needs of the body and soul, there are not many which deal with the functions and wounding of the human spirit. There is a great deal of literature available concerned with ministering into the physical, emotional and deliverance needs of a person, but very little about ministering into the broken, imprisoned or crushed spirit. This would seem to show that in this area, there is a marked lack of knowledge in the Body of Christ. This is very regrettable, especially when you consider that a person's spirit is the most vital part of their being. In fact, as I hope to show later, without the human spirit functioning properly, the body and the soul cannot.

Many people are walking around today with an apparently healthy body and soul, but with deep inner pain in their spirits. A number of these, after hearing my teaching on the subject on various training courses asked for it to be transcribed into written form. This booklet is the result. I hope that the following teaching will help us to recognise the nature of the human spirit; how it functions; what causes it to become wounded and how to minister God's healing.

Chapter 1

The Origin and Nature of the Human Spirit

The Origin of the Human Spirit

There are a number of basic questions concerning the origin, nature and work of the human spirit which we need to answer before we can begin to consider how the human spirit becomes wounded.

- What is the human spirit?
- Where does it come from?
- What is its purpose?
- Do we communicate with our spirit and if so how?

Whilst some of these questions are unanswerable, others are certainly within our reach, with the answers, I believe, being deeply rooted in God's word. I want us therefore to look at the scriptural evidence for the work and nature of the human spirit, before we look at how it becomes damaged. I will then give some pointers as to the way of ministering the healing love of Jesus into these wounds.

The first question to be asked would seem to be the most basic and the most obvious, as well as the most important. 'What is the source of the human spirit?' Or in other words, 'where does the human spirit come from?' The answer, as far as Scripture is concerned, is that our spirits come from God Himself. The prophet Zechariah tells us:

> *'Thus says the Lord, Who ... forms the spirit of man within him.'*   (Zechariah 12:1)

Just as God breathed the spirit into Adam in the beginning:

> *'Then the Lord God formed man from the dust of the ground and breathed into his nostrils the breath or spirit of life,'*   (Genesis 2:7)

so He forms the human spirit within each one of us.

The question then is: 'How does the human spirit get within man? Does God personally breathe the breath of life into each person in the womb?' It seems unlikely, but the answer, I'm afraid, is that we really don't know! As Ecclesiastes writes:

> *'As you know not what is the way of the wind, or how the spirit comes to the bones in the womb of a pregnant woman, even so you know not the work of God, Who does all.'* (Ecclesiastes 11:5)

What he is saying is that we are completely in the dark as to how the human spirit becomes part of a person. A number of scientists have speculated as to how it might happen, but the truth is that at this precise moment, we have to agree with Ecclesiastes. We honestly don't know. However what we do know is that our spirits come from God and will eventually return to God who gave them.

It is interesting to note that the writer of the book of Proverbs describes the human spirit as the:

> *'lamp of the Lord, searching all his innermost parts,'*   (Proverbs 20:2)

and John, in his gospel, states that Jesus is the:

> *'true Light (was then) coming into the world (the genuine, perfect, steadfast Light) that illumines every person.'*   (John 1:9)

It is as though Jesus Christ puts a flicker of light into each person as they are conceived, which then becomes their human spirit.

The Nature of the Human Spirit

We may not understand how or when we receive our human spirit but we do know that each one of us has one, as well as a body and a soul. It is that part of us which makes us completely different from every other person; the essential 'you', which is totally unique and special. That part of you which 'speaks' with others in a very deep and meaningful way. As you are probably aware, communication between individuals can take place on a number of different levels. We can communicate simply with our body: through our voices, facial expressions or touch; through our souls on an emotional level, by a sharing of our minds, or a combination of these methods. We also communicate through our spirits, that inner part of us that reaches out to other human beings on a much deeper level than through mere verbal, emotional or tactile expression.

Most of us will have some understanding of the nature of the soul area: our mind with which we think and reason; our emotions with which we feel and respond; our will with which we make decisions. We probably have an even greater understanding of our body and how that works, but what do we understand about the functions of our human spirit?

We have seen that, according to Scripture, God gives to every person who enters the human race a human spirit. This in itself raises a number of important questions. For example:

– What is the nature of the human spirit?
– What is its purpose?
– How does it function?

The Bible teaches us that we are made in the image of God. That our nature 'images' God's nature. In the Amplified Bible the word 'US', is in capital letters:

> *'Let Us (Father, Son and Holy Spirit) make mankind in Our image.'* (Genesis 1:26)

The Triune God is at work here, creating man after Their Own image, and springing from that discussion amongst the Godhead, that part of us which we call our human spirit took on the shape of the third person of the Trinity, the Holy Spirit. In other words our human spirit was created as a 'reflection', or 'image' of the Holy Spirit. The Father then implanted in man that part of the image of the Godhead (the Holy Spirit) which in man became known as the human spirit. Our human spirit 'images' the Holy Spirit and we need to look at the work and nature of the Holy Spirit in Scripture to see how it happens.

The Nature of the Holy Spirit

To understand then the **nature** of the **human spirit** we need to consider the **nature** of the **Holy Spirit**. Assuming that the imaging process takes place, what is true of the Holy Spirit will also, to a greater or lesser extent, be true of the human spirit. In Scripture the Holy Spirit's **nature** is defined by His different job functions, both primary and secondary. By primary, I mean the main role of the Holy Spirit, upon which the secondary roles rest and depend.

13

Chapter 2

The Primary Function of the Holy Spirit

The primary function of the Holy Spirit is to communicate life. As we read and study the Scriptures, we see that this is His main role. From Genesis to Revelation the word of God is full of examples of the Holy Spirit being the one who brings Life:

> *'The Spirit of God was moving (hovering, brooding) over the face of the waters.'* (Genesis 1:2)

Brooding, like a mother ready to bring forth life: which, in this instance, was the creation of the world. Another birth situation is recorded by the disciple Luke concerning the coming of Jesus. Luke 1:31 tells of the Angel Gabriel visiting Mary to tell her she was going to give birth to the Son of God. Mary quite rightly asks

> *'How can this be, since I have no ... husband?'*
> (Luke 1:34)

15

The answer which was given to her was:

> *'The Holy Spirit shall come upon you.'*
> (Luke 1:35)

The Angel Gabriel simply states that the Holy Spirit would bring life into Mary's womb; the very life of the second person of the Godhead: Jesus Christ, the Son of God.

Of course the prime example of the Holy Spirit as the Life-giver is that it is He who communicates the life of God into man's spirit. Scripture affirms that because of man's sin, our human spirits are dead towards God and therefore can have no living relationship with Him. The lines of communication are closed and Jesus says that without the Holy Spirit bringing life into our spirits, we can never come alive to God. We need to have our spirits reborn through the life-giving work of the Holy Spirit, in order to become a child of the Father, a member of God's family. Consider Jesus' discourse in John's Gospel with Nicodemus about the absolute necessity of being born of the Spirit:

> *'Jesus answered, I assure you, most solemnly I tell you, that unless a person is born again (anew, from above) he cannot ever see (know, be acquainted with, and experience) the Kingdom of God.'*
> (John 3:5)

Thus we can only enter the Kingdom of God when our spirit is brought to life by the Holy Spirit, otherwise we remain dead in our trespasses and sins. Through the Fall man died spiritually and the communication channels between God and man were broken. The Holy Spirit clears those communication barriers and brings our human spirit back to life:

> *'It is the Spirit who gives life.'*   (John 6:63)

However, it is even more glorious than that! He not only touches our spirit and brings it alive, but through His work, Christ actually indwells, permeates and makes His home within our human spirits:

> *'Christ within and among you, the Hope of (realizing the) Glory.'*   (Colossians 1:27)

This communication of life by the Holy Spirit is meant to be an ongoing process. We worship God with our spirit, and as we do so the Holy Spirit delights in pouring God's Life into us, life which brings refreshment, joy and vigour. For a number of years we ministered to people who had experienced difficulty with worshipping God, entering into His presence, or with 'knowing' Him as Father. It was assumed that it was an emotional problem, and that because of past bad parenting, they had developed a wrong view of God as a Father and therefore couldn't relate to Him in a right manner. So we would teach them the true picture of God as revealed in Scripture and through Jesus; we would

pray into their past hurt and pain and lead them
into repentance and forgiveness and we would
minister inner healing, but this was a largely unsuccessful ministry! The reason was that we were praying in the wrong area. We assumed the problem was
in the soul, that is in the emotions, when really the
problem was in the human spirit. We were led to
the passage in Romans 8:15, 16:

> *'For (the Spirit which) you have now received
> (is) not a spirit of slavery (to put you once more
> in bondage to fear, but you have received the
> Spirit of adoption (the Spirit producing sonship)
> in (the bliss of) which we cry, Abba (Father)!
> Father! The Spirit Himself (thus) testifies
> together with our own spirit (assuring us) that
> we are children of God.'*

The Holy Spirit witnesses with our spirit, not
with our emotions! That is where true life-giving
communication takes place. As the writer of John's
gospel puts it:

> *'God is a Spirit (a spiritual Being) and those
> who worship Him must worship Him in spirit
> and in truth.'*   (John 4:24)

That is why in worship it is possible to be feeling
very low emotionally, to be grief stricken or
depressed, and still come into the presence of God
and begin to worship with your spirit. That is the
reason why God can command that we praise Him

in all circumstances, because it is not reliant on how we feel but on our spirit's determination.

The Primary Function of the Human Spirit

Just as the Holy Spirit's primary job function is to communicate life to the human spirit, so in a like manner the human spirit's job function is to communicate life to our own body and soul. In fact when the human spirit ceases to do this and departs, **all** life departs and the body dies. This is why I refer to it as the primary role of the human spirit. The writer James affirms:

> *'the human body apart from the spirit is lifeless...'* (James 2:26)

So when the human spirit returns to God and ceases feeding life to the body and soul then, of course, the body dies and returns to the dust. As Ecclesiastes 12:7 puts it:

> *'Then shall the dust (out of which God made man's body) return to the earth as it was, and the spirit shall return to God Who gave it.'*

Jesus was so much in command of His spirit that He was able to say, on approaching death:

> *'"Father, into Your hands I commit My spirit!" And with these words, He expired.'* (Luke 23:46)

He truly chose to die, releasing His own human spirit to the Father. He laid down His life (His spirit), no one took it from Him.

However, it isn't only death that hinders the flow of life from our spirit into our body and soul, there are a number of other causes. I will show in a later chapter, the serious consequences to the rest of our nature when our human spirit is damaged and cannot fulfil this vital, primary, life-giving job function.

As well as supplying life to ourselves, we are also meant to communicate life to one another through our human spirits. God has given us the ability to touch each other not only physically and emotionally, but also with our spirits. Many of us have had the experience of meeting with someone for the very first time and feeling that we have known, and 'know' them, in a very deep way. We may have known other people for years and yet have never really 'known' them in any depth at all. What has happened? The difference is in the life-giving touch of the spirit. The cry of one lady's heart was: 'My husband will share about the news, the weather or the children, but never, never, never, does he share himself.' Their human spirits rarely touched and yet that was what her spirit longed for, and was created to enjoy.

This touching of spirits can be either 'life enhancing', or 'death producing'. Many folk are wounded and damaged in their spirits because they have had death, rather than life, fed into them continually. This is usually by key figures: parents, siblings, teachers, pastors. We may have experienced the situation when someone speaks good words to us with their mouths, but we receive a different message from their spirit.

So the primary function of our human spirit is to receive the Life of God from the Holy Spirit. This may be solely the created life or, as is true for the Christian, would also include the life of the 'new birth' (John 3:16). We then communicate that life to our own body and soul and thus to each other. We will consider in the next chapter the secondary functions of the Holy Spirit and therefore also of the human spirit.

Chapter 3

Secondary Functions of the Spirit – Part I

As well as the primary function discussed in chapter two, the Holy Spirit has a number of secondary functions. They are secondary, because they rely on the primary (which is communication of life) in order to exist. As we have seen, once this function ceases, so all of the following, secondary functions will cease.

1a. The Holy Spirit as a Communicator of Comfort and Strength

John 14, 15 and 16 talk about the Holy Spirit being a comforter and a strengthener. In these three chapters Jesus speaks continually to the disciples about the Holy Spirit drawing alongside them. He reminds them that He is going to have to leave them, but that they would not be left comfortless. Indeed He assures them:

> *'I will ask the Father, and He will give you another Comforter (Counsellor, Helper, Intercessor, Advocate, Strengthener and Standby) that He may remain with you forever – The Spirit of Truth.'*   (John 14:16, 17a)

The Holy Spirit would be a *'parakletos'*, one who would draw alongside as an encourager. What a wonderful promise of strength, help and encouragement is available from the Holy Spirit, not only to the first disciples, but to all those who receive Him. For His job, His purpose, His reason for being, is to come alongside the believer.

1b. The Human Spirit as a Communicator of Comfort and Strength

In like manner, the human spirit, as well as communicating life, is also meant to communicate comfort and strength to the body and soul, as a means of sustaining and encouraging us. When we are weary, disconsolate or grief-stricken it is the job of the human spirit to lift and encourage us. The psalmist knew this when he wrote:

> *'Why are thou cast down, O my inner self? And why should you moan over me and be disquieted within me? Hope in God.'*   (Psalm 42:5)

In other words the psalmist is telling the spirit to do its job! Paul reminds us that the human spirit is also meant to encourage and comfort others. He writes that he is full of joy at seeing Titus because:

'you have all set his mind at rest, soothing and refreshing his spirit.'

2a. The Holy Spirit as a Communicator of Truth

The Holy Spirit is the one who reveals the hidden things of God, the one who will communicate the truth of God to man. Isaiah 40:13–14 reminds us that no one can teach God anything or find out what God is like by his own means. Jesus, teaching His disciples this important truth, asserts:

'When He, the Spirit of Truth (the Truth – giving Spirit) comes, He will guide you into all Truth.' (John 16:13)

It is the work of the Holy Spirit to reveal the truth about God. One of the ways in which He does this is through the inspiration of the Scriptures. As Peter asserts in his second letter:

'No prophecy of Scripture is (a matter) of any personal or private or special interpretation (loosening, solving). For no prophecy ever originated because some man willed it (to do so – it never came by human impulse), but men spoke from God who were borne along (moved and impelled) by the Holy Spirit.' (2 Peter 1:20, 21)

This work of the Holy Spirit is for a specific purpose. 2 Timothy 3:16, 17 says:

> *'Every Scripture is God-breathed (given by His inspiration) and profitable for instruction, for reproof and conviction of sin, for correction of error and discipline in obedience, (and) for training in righteousness (in holy living, in conformity to God's will in thought, purpose and action).'*

The Holy Spirit also reveals the mind of God to the believer. As Paul writes to the Corinthians, the wisdom and blessings of God have now been revealed:

> *'God has unveiled and revealed them by and through His Spirit, for the (Holy) Spirit searches diligently, exploring and examining everything, even sounding the profound and bottomless things of God (the divine counsels and things hidden and beyond man's scrutiny).'*
> (1 Corinthians 12:10)

The place where the Holy Spirit reveals truth, to the individual, is within his human spirit. This is where guidance is received, and because we are all open to error this will need testing by more mature Christians and lined up continually with the Scriptures. The same is true of the gifts of the Holy Spirit. Words of knowledge, wisdom, prophecy, interpretation of tongues etc., are all placed in the human spirit by the Holy Spirit, and will need to be judged and discerned by the Body of Christ. We are encouraged to test everything especially with regard to prophecy, where we have been told to:

> *'pay attention and weigh and discern what is said.'* (1 Corinthians 14:29)

However, testing everything doesn't mean that we test the truth of God with our minds alone, and if the gift does not line up with commonsense we disregard it. This can often happen with the gifts of the Spirit. Our mind can become the 'censor' of the human spirit. We receive a gift from the Holy Spirit, maybe a word of knowledge concerning someone for whom we are praying. The Holy Spirit has placed that 'truth' into our spirits, in order for us to communicate it into the life of the person in need. However our mind moves forward into action. We think: 'That cannot be a true word of knowledge, it doesn't make sense,' or 'That cannot possibly be a prophetic word, it is too ridiculous.' This censorship of the mind over the spirit means that we do not speak out the truth which the Holy Spirit has given to us. In other words we:

> *'quench (suppress or subdue) the (Holy) Spirit.'* (1 Thessalonians 5:19)

We need to constantly remember that:

> *'the natural, nonspiritual man does not accept or welcome or admit into his heart the gifts and*

teachings and revelations of the Spirit of God, for they are folly (meaningless nonsense) to him; and he is incapable of knowing them (of progressively recognizing, understanding, and becoming better acquainted with them) because they are spiritually discerned and estimated and appreciated.' (1 Corinthians 2:14)

We are all in the process of having our carnal nature changed into the fully spiritual being, who has the 'mind of Christ' and until that is accomplished, we need to remember Paul's warning that the 'unspiritual' man cannot understand or judge the 'spiritual'.

2b. The Human Spirit as a Communicator of Truth

Because we 'image' or 'mirror' the Holy Spirit, there is a part of the human spirit whose job function is to reveal truth, truth in the inward parts. It is also the place where we receive our 'knowing' and our 'intuition' about God and others.

'For what person perceives (knows and understands) what passes through a man's thoughts except the man's own spirit within him?'
(1 Corinthians 2:11)

This 'knowing' begins even in the womb. Luke records an amazing statement concerning Mary's visit to her cousin Elizabeth, who was six months pregnant. As Mary arrives at her house, Luke says:

> *'when Elizabeth heard Mary's greeting, the baby leaped in her womb,'* (Luke 1:41)

and just in case we didn't receive it the first time, Luke repeats this staggering truth as Elizabeth cries out:

> *'For behold, the instant the sound of your saluta-tion reached my ears, the baby in my womb leaped for joy.'* (Luke 1:44)

Why was the baby leaping? Because there was an intuitive 'knowing' by John the Baptist, whilst in the womb of his mother, that he was in the presence of Jesus the Son of God, who at that moment in time, was within the womb of Mary. Where did John receive this revelation? I believe that he received it from the Holy Spirit who placed it into his human spirit. Thus the baby leapt for joy as Elizabeth was:

> *'filled with and controlled by the Holy Spirit.'*
> (Luke 1:41b)

He (the Holy Spirit), prompted her to speak the words which were an enormous encouragement and strength to Mary at that very difficult time:

> *'Blessed (favoured of God) above all other*
> *women are you! And blessed (favoured of God)*
> *is the Fruit of your womb.'*   (Luke 1:42)

These words, which were spoken from Elizabeth's spirit straight into Mary's spirit, caused her in turn to proclaim:

> *'My spirit rejoices in God my Saviour.'*
>   (Luke 1:47)

An amazing example of the job function of the Holy Spirit working with the job function of the human spirit, revealing and communicating encouragement, life and truth both to the person, and through that person, into the spirit of another, in this case Mary the mother of Jesus.

This intuitive knowing or revealing aspect of the human spirit continues throughout a person's life. Peter knew in his spirit that Jesus was:

> *'the Christ, the Son of the living God.'*
>   (Matthew 16:16)

We are told that this was a revelation to him from the Father in heaven; in other words from the Holy Spirit into Peter's spirit. We 'know' others and 'know' the truth about others through our spirits. Someone may speak pleasant, kind and seemingly upbuilding words to you, but in your spirit you are reading a different message. You feel uneasy. Why? Because with their words they are saying one thing, but in their spirits they are saying something totally different and you are reading their spirit. They speak or communicate 'life' with their lips, but 'death' with their spirit.

3a. The Holy Spirit as the One who Convicts

It is also the Holy Spirit's job function to bring men and women under conviction of sin and of their need of a Saviour:

> *'And when He comes, He will convict and convince the world and bring demonstration to it about sin.'* (John 16:8)

It is impossible for a preacher or an evangelist to convict a person of their need of the Saviour. That is the job function of the Holy Spirit. We can bring them under condemnation; only He can bring them to conviction. Those involved with the great revivals knew the truth of this and leant heavily upon this aspect of the Holy Spirit's work. Most Christians are all too aware of the convicting work of the Holy Spirit within their lives and it would seem that the nearer a person draws to God, the more conscious they become of their sin.

3b. The Human Spirit as the One who Convicts

In a similar manner the human spirit is also meant

to convict a person (through their conscience) of right and wrong. If it is fulfilling its job function then the spirit keeps the body and soul in line with God's law, which Scripture says is written in every one's heart:

> *'They (the Gentiles) show that the essential requirements of the Law are written in their hearts and are operating there, with which their consciences (sense of right and wrong) also bear witness.'*
> (Romans 2:15)

So, if we have the law of God within our hearts and one of the functions of our spirit is that of bringing conviction, then we have no excuse for sin when we stand before God, whether we are Christians or not. It is possible, though, for the conscience to be rendered inactive, because it has become hardened against God's law:

> *'Today, if you would hear His voice and when you hear it, do not harden your hearts.'*
> (Hebrews 4:7)

We need to constantly allow the Holy Spirit to convict us of any hardening towards sin. We also need to allow Him to examine us as to whether our conscience has become defiled and therefore cannot fulfil this very important role of acting like a 'spiritual policeman'. We shall look in a later chapter as to the reasons for a defiled spirit, and how to minister cleansing and wholeness in order for our spirits to become sensitive and so fulfil this very important role.

4a. The Holy Spirit as a Creator

Another function of the Holy Spirit is that of being involved with acts of creation. We have already noted that the Holy Spirit was present at the creation of the world, as He worked alongside the Father and the Son, in bringing into being the universe as we know it. Job goes further and affirms that the Holy Spirit was not only involved in the creation of the world, He was actually involved in the creation of 'me'.

'The Spirit of God has made me.'   (Job 33:4)

Job was no doubt basing that conviction on the story in Genesis 2, where it is written that God:

> *'formed man from the dust of the ground and breathed into his nostrils the breath or spirit of life, and man became a living being.'*
> (Genesis 2:7)

This is very reminiscent of the time when Jesus appeared to his disciples after the resurrection and:

> *'breathed on them and said to them, "Receive (admit) the Holy Spirit!"'*   (John 20:22)

Here we are seeing the Holy Spirit present and involved in a new creation, which was ultimately fulfilled at Pentecost; the creation of the Church, the Body of Christ.

4b. The Human Spirit as a Creator

To a lesser extent the human spirit is also meant to be a vehicle for creativity, the difference being that our creativity is a 'secondary creativity', relying and drawing inspiration from God's creation. Nevertheless, with that proviso, there is a function of man's spirit which is able to create. The majority of inspirational and beautiful music was created first in the human spirit of the composer and then flowed out of his spirit onto the page. That is why when we are listening to a wonderful composition, we are moved in our 'spirit'. The music, which began in another spirit, is speaking to our spirit. The same could be said about beautiful and moving works of art and explains, to some extent, why men and women will give anything to possess a certain picture, book or artefact. They are reaching out in their spirits to that which was first created in another human spirit.

This creative function, I believe, is also the reason why some people have a deep desire and longing to be out walking on the mountains; crossing deep valleys or simply standing and beholding a rushing mighty waterfall. They are desirous of feeding that creative area of their human spirit. Such manifestations of nature are to the spirit what a drink of clear cold water would be to a dry and thirsty man.

Chapter 4

Secondary Functions of the Spirit – Part II

5a. The Holy Spirit as the One who Empowers

'But truly I (Micah) am full of power of the Spirit of the Lord.' (Micah 3:8)

The Old Testament is full of examples of men and women who were empowered by the Holy Spirit: Elisha (2 Kings 2:14), Samson (Judges 14:6) and Gideon (Judges 6:34), to name but a few. The Holy Spirit is the empowerer, the one who strengthens the Body of Christ. Indeed Jesus warns His disciples not to go running around in their own strength, but to wait in Jerusalem, in order that they may receive the power of the Holy Spirit. He promises His disciples and future believers:

'you shall receive power (ability, efficiency, and might) when the Holy Spirit has come upon you,' (Acts 1:8)

and we need only to read the book of Acts to see how much and how effectively the Holy Spirit empowered the early Church. History confirms that He has continued his work down the ages, empowering and strengthening each new generation of the Church.

5b. The Human Spirit as the One who Empowers

Similarly the human spirit is meant to provide power and strength to the body and soul.

> *'The strong spirit of a man sustains him in bodily pain or trouble.'* (Proverbs 18:14)

The stronger our human spirits are, the more able they will be to fulfil this role. Many heroic tales are told of people who have supernatural strength under impossible circumstances. How do they do it, we ask? I suggest one reason might be that their spirit is performing this function in a superhuman way. Or consider those going through a very difficult time with many friends praying for them. They feel strong and able to cope much better than they ever imagined. What is happening? I suggest that those who are praying are, in their spirit, strengthening the body and soul of their friend in need.

A lady wrote to me recently concerning the help her friends were to her as she was going through a very difficult time. Her marriage was not good, her sons were verbally abusing her, she felt abandoned by almost everyone and was experiencing great rejection. She says: 'I was unable to get up off my couch. I could not even pray. I had friends who took my needs to the Lord. As long as they prayed I could function, but when they stopped, I could feel my strength being drained away.'

What was happening? I believe that they were fulfilling this role of pouring strength into her spirit through their prayers. The Holy Spirit was interceding for her through them and thus her body and soul were strengthened until she herself was strong enough in spirit to pray for herself.

The question which then arises is: 'How is the human spirit strengthened in order for it to fulfil this very important function?' I would suggest that for the Christian, there are a number of ways. As we have seen, we can be strengthened through the prayers of our friends in the Body of Christ; through the prayers of Jesus, who is always interceding for each one of us at the right hand of God; through worship; through reading God's Word and through speaking in tongues. Paul writes that this 'edifies' the Christian, it builds him up. The most vital way for our spirit to be strengthened however is through the prayers of the Holy Spirit who:

> *'Himself goes to meet our supplication and pleads in our behalf with unspeakable yearnings and groanings too deep for utterance.'*
>
> (Romans 8:26)

I would also suggest that when the Holy Spirit prays for us the job function of the Holy Spirit and the job function of the human spirit are linked together, like cogs in a wheel. We then draw from Him the power, strength and comfort which we need. It was said of both John the Baptist and Jesus that they:

> *'became strong in spirit.'*
>
> (Luke 1:80a; Luke 2:40a)

I believe this was through the empowering of their spirits by the Holy Spirit.

6a. The Holy Spirit as a Facilitator

The Holy Spirit is also a facilitator, the means by which God's plans are translated into action. For example, as we have seen, the Holy Spirit was the one who brought into being God's plans for the creation of the world:

> *'The earth was without form and an empty waste, and darkness was upon the face of the very great deep. The Spirit of God was moving (hovering, brooding) over the face of the water;'*
>
> (Genesis 1:2b)

and also of the Incarnation:

> *'His mother Mary had been promised in marriage to Joseph, before they came together,*

she was found to be pregnant (through the power) of the Holy Spirit.'   (Matthew 1:18)

The Holy Spirit enabled the work of Jesus to be so effective:

'But if it is by the Spirit of God that I drive out demons, then the Kingdom of God has come upon you.'   (Matthew 12:28)

Jesus only began His public ministry after He was baptized with the Holy Spirit (Luke 3:22). Indeed Luke tells us that it was the Holy Spirit who controlled Jesus and led Him into the wilderness (Luke 4:1) after which:

'Jesus went back full of and under the power of the (Holy) Spirit into Galilee.'   (Luke 4:14)

The Holy Spirit was also the facilitator who enabled Jesus to rise from the dead. According to Romans 8:11:

'And if the Spirit of Him Who raised up Jesus from the dead dwells in you, (then) He Who raised up Christ Jesus from the dead will also restore to life your mortal (short-lived, perishable) bodies through His Spirit Who dwells in you.'

Isn't that wonderful? It is the Holy Spirit who will raise us to life, just as He did with Jesus.

6b. The Human Spirit as a Facilitator

I would suggest that our human spirits also 'mirror' or 'image' the Holy Spirit in being facilitators of God's purposes, to a lesser extent. It is, of course, only the Holy Spirit's work within and through the human spirit that brings in the Kingdom of God. Nevertheless we, as part of the Body of Christ, have a role to play, which is to be led by the Holy Spirit and allow Him to work though us (that is through our spirit) in order that we might 'work the works of God'. It is in our spirits that we receive the fruit and the gifts of the Holy Spirit, which God means to flow through us, in order to bring evangelism, healing and deliverance to a needy world.

So in summary, we can see that the human spirit mirrors or images the nature of the Holy Spirit and thus has similar primary and secondary job functions, the primary functions being: to receive life in the human spirit via the Holy Spirit; to communicate with and worship the Creator; to communicate and sustain the life of the body and soul; to communicate and interact with others. I call these the primary functions because without communication of life to the body (physical) and to the spirit (spiritual), death reigns and the other functions cease or are limited. Therefore the other functions rely to some greater or lesser extent upon the primary function.

The secondary functions of the human spirit are: to comfort and encourage my body and soul and that of others; to understand and know the things of God and man, through revelation or intuition; to bring conviction through the conscience; to take part in creative activities; to empower and strengthen my body and soul and that of others; to allow the spirit to be used by the Holy Spirit to facilitate the plans of God and so assist in establishing the Kingdom of God.

Chapter 5

A Model to Meet the World

I would like to suggest to you a new way of approaching the world, which for the Christian who wants to be led by the Holy Spirit is really the only way to live. The suggestion is that we ought to be meeting other people and situations not primarily with our bodies and souls but with our spirits. What do I mean by that? Paul writes to the Christians at Thessalonica that we are spirit, soul and body (1 Thessalonians 5:23). Very often we turn that around and quote it as 'body, soul and spirit', because that is our experience of approaching the world. We meet people with our bodies first, then our souls (mind, emotions and will) and then maybe, just maybe, we touch spirits. However, as Paul knew, we are first and foremost spiritual beings who need to learn how to approach others 'spirit first'.

In order to put that into practice we need to change our thinking and follow the lead of Jesus who continually met people and situations 'spiritually' first. For example He was already spiritually attuned at the age of twelve, when He was found:

> *'in My Father's house and (occupied) about My Father's business?'* (Luke 2:49)

He spiritually read the situation of the woman taken in adultery and responded accordingly, to give an accurate summing up of the universality of sin; He was spiritually aware of the pain and wounding in the woman who had bled for twelve years and dealt not only with her physical problem, but her inner isolation and unrest as well.

> *'Daughter, your faith (your confidence and trust in Me) has made you well! Go (enter) into peace (untroubled, undisturbed well-being).'*
> (Luke 8:43–48)

Jesus was truly:

> *'led by the Spirit of God.'* (Romans 8:14)

For us to do likewise the human spirit needs to be in 'spiritual alignment' with the Holy Spirit. He will then feed life; comfort and encouragement; truth and knowledge; conviction of right and wrong; strength and power into our human spirit, and because we have aligned our spirit with Him, we take these attributes and through the same job functions of our spirit, we feed them into our own body and soul and out into the world. Thus we find that we are 'led' by the Holy Spirit. He enables us to meet people spirit to spirit and as the water of life flows out of our 'bellies', so others are touched and changed by Him.

The only drawback to this way of living is that it makes you very vulnerable, especially if you are a sensitive person. This is because when you open your spirit (your 'inner being') to someone else, you risk your spirit being trampled on. In the Jewish Temple the Holy of Holies is on the inside, the Inner Sanctuary next and then the Outer Court. The Holy of Holies is like the human spirit. It is that inner part of a person which needs to be guarded and treasured, but ready to be revealed to those who wish to draw near and meet, spirit to spirit.

When the human spirit has been brought alive to God, indwelt by the Spirit of God and functioning the way He intended, then we live a life which is full and satisfying. The problem arises, however, when the spirit becomes sick and the functions become impaired. There are a lot of people who are not only damaged in their emotions, or in their bodies, but they also carry deep wounds in their spirits. Nelson Mandela returned to visit Robben Island where he was in jail for nineteen years. The trip came on the fourth anniversary of his release from prison. As he shared some of the memories of those times, the pain inevitably seeped through. 'Wounds that can't be seen are more painful than those that can be seen and cured by a doctor,' said

Mr Mandela. 'One of the saddest moments in my life in prison was the death of my mother. The next shattering experience was the death of my eldest son in a car accident.' He was forbidden from attending either funeral. Such wounds go deep.

The questions which then arise are:
- How does our spirit become sick?
- What are the causes of damage?
- How does this damage affect the functions of the spirit?
- What are the symptoms and what are the remedies for a sick spirit?

In other words 'How do we minister into this vital area?'

Chapter 6

Areas of Damage – A Timid Spirit

Now that we have seen the origin, nature and function of the human spirit, let us consider what happens when it becomes sick or damaged in any way. In order to do that we will look at the various kinds of damage that may occur.

A Timid and Fearful Spirit

Many people limp through their lives with what I have called a 'timid spirit'. They appear to be frightened of every new situation and even of life itself, although as Scripture reminds us:

> *'God did not give us a spirit of timidity (of cowardice, of craven and cringing and fawning fear).'* (2 Timothy 1:7)

Whilst some people suffer from varied emotional fears, for example fear of travel, fear of the dark or fear of spiders, those with a 'timid spirit' suffer non-specific but a rather generalised, all-pervasive fear and anxiety about life itself. This goes much deeper, springing not from their emotions, but from their spirits.

What are the hallmarks of a person with a timid spirit? They will be the kind of person who will continually need lots of reassurance and love. You may feed much affection into them, but this will quickly disappear down a bottomless hole. They will often draw back from new situations, desiring to keep in the background as much as possible. One lady we shared with and ministered to was a church organist. Every Sunday she had to face the congregation as she made her way to the organ to play for the service. It felt, in her own words, 'like dying a thousand deaths'. The distance she had to walk was approximately six metres, but to her it was the equivalent of climbing Mount Everest. Her timid spirit shrivelled up at the thought of it, and she felt like taking flight physically. It was sheer grit and determination which made her fulfil what she saw as her duty.

Very often they will have a guarded approach to life and won't come out to meet you. You may make contact with their outer being, but they will never reveal their soul or their inner spirit. They are unsure as to whether life, or people, can ever really be good to them or can be trusted not to wound them further. They fear and expect the worst. They live with the expectation that life will hit them in the back and knock them flat on their face. They may be the kind of person who has a high degree of sensitivity to criticism, which they see when none is intended, and read into other people's body language unspoken disapproval of themselves. They keep their timid spirit closed and locked against others, because they are terrified that they are going to be hurt and wounded even more than they have been. They are like the little canary who refuses to fly, because it fears that flying will lead to death.

Causes of a Timid Spirit

Usually the root of a timid spirit will be found in some trauma in early life, for example like the child who was continually sick at birth. After a number of x-rays and examinations, it was discovered that she was born with her intestines the wrong way round, which was why she couldn't digest her food. The child had an emergency operation when she was three weeks old and the surgeon very wisely warned the parents that 'new situations' might cause the child some fear and anxiety. He was right. She, as a result of that trauma, became 'timid' in her spirit. Thankfully the Lord, over the years, has brought a great measure of healing to her.

The traumas could include any pre- or post-birth experiences. If a pregnant woman receives a terrible shock whilst carrying her baby in the womb, the baby may pick up the timidity of the mother in its own spirit. A very difficult and traumatic birth could be another source. Sometimes timidity of spirit can be the result of the death of a parent at a young age, an accident or separation from the parents for any reason. In fact whenever security is perceived to be removed from the child, it can have this adverse reaction in its young spirit.

It is also possible for there to be a generational problem, where there may be a tendency for timidity of spirit to be passed down the family line. This can usually be traced to some incident in the past which has had a deep and lasting effect upon the family. One gentleman we ministered to had a great grandfather who had been in a violent argument with a neighbour and was consequently murdered. The subsequent men in the family all suffered from timidity of spirit.

Functions Impaired

The functions of the human spirit which are impaired here are: communication with others which becomes very inhibited; and an inability to comfort or empower their own body and soul, therefore leaving them unable to strengthen the spirit and soul of others in need.

Ministering to the Timid Spirit

In every kind of damage to the human spirit, you will need to be aware that the memories and pain which has caused the wounding, will need to be exposed and healed. So we must be continually looking for the root of the wounding. However, for this to be done, the person will need to come to a place of security with you, for they will not share their innermost being until they feel that they can trust you and that you are, indeed, a trustworthy person. This takes time. When you have gained their trust, there are a number of questions which will need to be asked, such as:

– What happened in the past to cause this timidity of spirit?
– Does the timidity show itself in any specific situations, and if so, what are they?
– Did your parents have a similar problem? (Here you are looking for a generational timidity as instanced above.)

Because Satan takes advantage of the dark and wounded places in our lives, we have to be aware that the demonic may also need to be dealt with, if and when it arises. We will take this as understood and therefore not repeat it each time we consider ministering into the wounded spirit.

Once we have discovered the root, we then begin to pray under the guidance of the Holy Spirit, asking Him to bring to the surface any buried traumatic memory and praying through it. We ask that He will be the bridge between the memory and the pain, in order for the hurt, shame or any other emotions to be released to the Lord. We need to specifically release the fear and pray into their spirits the *'shalom'*, the peace of Jesus. We then need to teach the person the importance of being:

'transformed (changed) by the (entire) renewal of your mind (by its new deals and its new attitude).'   (Romans 12:2)

They will need to learn how to work with the Holy Spirit, in order to change their behaviour patterns and attitudes from fear to complete confidence in Him. They need to grasp with their spirit the fact that He is, and will be, their strength and encourager. This comes through a revelation from the Holy Spirit into their spirits, into that 'intuitive' part, which grasps spiritual truth.

Summary

1. Take time to build up **trust** with the person.
2. Always look for the **root** of the 'timidity'.
3. Pray and allow the Holy Spirit to minister into the **roots**.
4. Teach the person the importance of renewing their **mind**.

Chapter 7

Areas of Damage –
An Imprisoned Spirit

Some people are walking around with their human spirit bound and chained, as though it were in a dank, dark, depressing prison. They live within themselves, simply existing in a cage, with iron bars around them. This inhibits freedom and causes their spirit to sink into the gloom of despair and despondency. They never, or rarely, know the joy of fun and laughter, creativity and exuberance. The psalmist knew something of that experience when he cried out that the enemy:

> 'has made me to dwell in dark places as those who have been long dead. Therefore is my spirit overwhelmed and faints within me (wrapped in gloom),'　　　　　　　　　　　(Psalm 143:3)

and longs for God to

> 'Bring my life out of prison.'　　　(Psalm 142:7)

The one with an imprisoned spirit is doubly bound. He is bound by the chains which hold him and the iron bars which inhibit him. The chains I see as the **cause** of his imprisonment, whilst the bars I see as the **result** of that imprisonment.

Causes of an Imprisoned Spirit

Let us consider the chains or causes first. As with the timid spirit, any traumatic situation can imprison the spirit. A lady we ministered to was put straight into an incubator when she was born. (Her mother was seriously ill and needed to be attended to first.) The baby was presumed dead by the doctor and it was some hours, if not a whole day, before they had finished attending to the mother and turned their attention to the baby.

She had been left alone without food or nurture for what must have seemed, to the baby, a very long time. The result was that her spirit, as well as her body, became entrapped in that incubator. She developed an 'imprisoned spirit'. The details of her birth were relayed to her by her mother who affirmed that from the moment she was able to pick her daughter up, she would withdraw and turn away from her.

Because we are spirit, soul and body, any kind of physical or emotional bondage can cause the spirit to become imprisoned too. For example, physical addictions, such as alcohol or drug abuse, anorexia or bulimia will have a repercussion in the spirit.

Any kind of emotional control or domination can have the same result, like the child who, at three years old, waited outside her parent's workplace for them to finish their work shift. She was terrified of moving, standing and feeling like a stone statue, both inside and out, because mother had said, 'Stand there and don't move or the bogey-man will get you!'

If a person has been starved in any way this will have a repercussion in their spirit. The starvation may have been of food (as with the baby placed in the incubator and presumed dead) or of affection, or even protection. Starvation, of any kind, dries up the spirit. Parents who have run a home based on a very strict regime, such as the father who was a sergeant major, both on the parade ground and at home!, will cause the spirit of the child to become very withdrawn and isolated. Sometimes Christians suffering from strict legalism in their church, or very heavy shepherding, will need ministry into their imprisoned spirit, as well as into spiritual abuse. They will have had heavy chains of legalism imposed upon them, from which they will need to be set free.

The Results of an Imprisoned Spirit

Because the one whose spirit is in prison has been badly hurt, they place bars of protection around themselves in order that the hurt will not grow more intense. The iron bars may be many and varied, but in my experience **isolation** is normally one of the key ones. This is usually self-imposed, in that they prefer their own company. 'Nobody is going to get close to me, and I won't allow myself to get close to others' is a description of their inner life. The path of solitude is much more preferable than that of being in fellowship with others, because they do not know how to relate. They are likely to be the 'lone wolf' in your congregation. Linked with this is the iron bar of **control**, in that they like to control their own patch. It makes them feel much safer. Very often they will try to control their families as well. The bar of **legalism** is a lifestyle which suits the person with an imprisoned spirit and sometimes a Christian will find themselves drawn to a very legalistic fellowship for that very reason.

Denial and **poverty** are the final bars which keep them in prison. They literally feel that they shouldn't have anything good or enjoyable. They are unworthy. The 'bread and water diet', or the 'hair-shirt regime' is all that they are worthy of obtaining. This is not a reasoned, thought out, point of view, it is something that has been seared into their very spirit. They feel guilty if they are enjoying themselves and very quickly find a reason to stop. They must live on the minimum. One lady, who was given lots of beautiful presents by her family for Christmas or birthdays would put them to one side and give them away to others throughout the year. She didn't feel worthy to receive such gifts.

Functions Impaired

For the person with the imprisoned spirit the primary function of communication is seriously impaired. Consider someone trying to communicate through iron bars or, as sometimes happens in a prison, trying to talk through a glass panel. This is how it can feel to the one with their spirit in prison. Often they will feel completely misunderstood or misheard. This is because the communication function is not working properly. Within a marriage, if both partners have imprisoned spirits, they end up not communicating, but shouting at each other, with neither understanding the other!

The secondary function of revelation and intuition is also seriously distorted. They cannot see the world, God, or other people with a right perspective, just as our bodies are distorted if we view ourselves in the funfair mirrors at Blackpool! The creative role is also impaired; it is not free to soar, because it has leaden boots on!

Ministering to the Imprisoned Spirit

First you must look for, and minister into, the reasons and roots of the chains that bind them, asking questions such as:
- What caused your spirit to become so locked away and twisted?
- What prompted that poverty of outlook?
- What caused your joylessness?

The Holy Spirit may give words of knowledge

concerning their past. He may bring into their minds a memory or a picture, which will reveal the source of the problem, like the word of knowledge which was given, concerning a gentleman we were ministering to. The word was 'coffin'. The Holy Spirit used this word to reveal the root of his problem. Evidently, when he was a young child of three, his mother had left him with an uncle for the day. The uncle had become ill during the course of the morning, leaving the young child very frightened and vulnerable. He had spent the major part of the day trying to attract attention by banging on the window or trying to shake his uncle into consciousness. The result was that he felt trapped as though he were in a coffin. What happened to him physically had deep repercussions in his spirit.

After you have discovered the roots of the imprisonment, you will need to pray through them, breaking the chains; the same will need to be done concerning the iron bars, which have been erected to protect them from any more pain. They will need, by an act of their will, to choose to take those iron bars down, repent for trying to protect themselves and choose to allow God to protect them in the future. Each bar will need to be broken specifically, through the power of the Holy Spirit, always being aware that the demonic may be present, for he loves to work in the dark.

The person will come to a point in ministry where they will need to walk out of their prison, just as Lazarus had to choose to *'come forth'*, when Jesus called him out. A lifetime of habit structures will need to be laid to rest. Take time to encourage them to:

> *'be transformed (changed) by the (entire) renewal of your mind,'* (Romans 12:2)

and to alter their behaviour patterns as the Lord points them out. Jesus can call their spirit back to life, but they have to remove the bars and bandages which they have put around their spirit. They need to see that they are a child of God with a right to enjoy life, a right to joy, freedom and creativity.

You will also need to feed and nurture their spirit, little by little replacing what has been missing, fun things as well as spiritual. Good parents automatically feed their child's spirit. It is the first thing mothers do when they feed their baby at the breast. They pour not only food into the baby, but love, pride and joy as well. Just look at the smile on the face of a new mother. This smile and pride increases when father notes the first tooth, the first words, the first faltering, stumbling steps, all filling the heart with joy and bringing that spirit to spirit communication which is so essential to the baby's development. 'You are wonderful.' 'You are the most amazing child that has ever been born.' 'There is no child like our child!' Of course there is a reassessment later! But the child's spirit has been fed and nurtured at a very important stage in its life.

The person with an imprisoned spirit has never known that nurturing of the spirit (not always because of the fault of the parents) but nevertheless is starved on the inside. Such children don't know that they are wonderful, that they are precious and valuable. Someone in the Body of Christ has to be available to feed such truth into their spirits. Remember to give the person permission to enjoy themselves, reminding them that healing may be a slow process, but that as they work with God, gradually they will begin to walk out into a greater freedom, and know the truth which Charles Wesley wrote:

> 'Long my imprisoned spirit lay
> Fast bound in sin and nature's night;
> Thine eye diffused a quickening ray –
> I woke, the dungeon filled with light;
> My chains fell off, my heart was free,
> I rose, went forth, and followed thee.'
>
> (Methodist Hymn Book)

Summary

1. Look for and minister into the **roots**.
2. Lead them in **repentance** for erecting the iron bars.
3. Get them to **choose** to take the iron bars down.
4. **Holy Spirit** led ministry.
5. Remind them that their wrong **habit structures** will need breaking.
6. Feed and **nurture** their spirit.

Chapter 8

Areas of Damage – A Crushed Spirit

The third area of damage to the spirit is that of having a crushed and bruised spirit, or a heavy, burdened and failing spirit. Scripture lays the blame for this on Satan:

> 'He (the enemy) has crushed my life down to the ground.' (Psalm 143:3)

Some people seem to be continually grieving on the inside. They have very little self-affirmation and almost no self-worth. If you ask such a person what they think about themselves, you will read self-rejection in every sentence of their answer. There will probably be a sense of weariness and despair in their body language. Because their spirit is crushed it cannot do its job function of sustaining, strengthening and encouraging their body and soul. Very often their face will show continual sadness, with tears always near to the surface.

For people with a crushed and heavy spirit, suicide may be constantly on their minds: 'What's the use?' 'What is the point?' 'I might as well give up.' 'I'd be better off dead.' Self-pity may take root, as in the case of Elijah when threatened by Jezebel:

> *'And I, I only, am left, and they seek my life, to destroy it.'* (1 Kings 19:14b)

Sometimes people who have a crushed spirit will resort to anorexia or bulimia, because the role of supporting and strengthening the body becomes too onerous and the spirit gives up. It begins to seek to destroy that which it is meant to support. The good news, as the prophet Isaiah reminds us, is that God will give:

> *'the garment (expressive) of praise instead of a heavy, burdened, and failing spirit.'*
> (Isaiah 61:3)

Causes of a Crushed Spirit

One of the main causes of a crushed spirit is inappropriate burden bearing. Many people are called upon to walk through life with responsibilities, which are far too onerous for their age or experience, like the little girl whom I taught. She had the responsibility, at the age of five, of getting herself ready for school every morning, her mother being unable or unwilling, to get out of bed because of late nights spent with her friends. However Helen (as I will call her) not only had to feed, wash and dress herself, she also had to do the same for her three year old brother. She was then responsible for taking him to nursery, before making her way, wearily, to school by herself.

Considering her young age, it was not surprising that even then she was showing signs of a crushed, heavy and burdened spirit. Helen had never known protection, only burdens placed upon her. Therefore the natural joy and exuberance of childhood was sadly missing. Her shoulders would be stooped, her face expressive of deep sadness, and it took most of the morning to encourage her to relax and play with her friends.

Any form of manipulation and control from authority figures can cause crushing of the spirit. Teachers may do this unthinkingly, as they place a sensitive child in front of a class and insist on them performing! As well as physically cringing, very often the spirit will cringe too. Harsh leadership or powerful words can bring a crushing of the human spirit, as was the case with Elijah. We see him, in 2 Kings 18, fearlessly calling down the fire of the Lord on the prophets of Baal. In 2 Kings 19, we see him running for his life, because of the threatening words of Jezebel, who sent this message to him:

> *'So let the gods do to me, and more also, if I make not your life as the life of one of them (the Baal prophets who were dead) by this time (tomorrow).'* (1 Kings 19:2)

These words were enough to send Elijah into a spiral of despair. In fact he was so frightened and crushed in spirit that he ran for eighty miles, until he was well out of the territory of Jezebel. Words are very powerful and they can so easily wound, bruise and crush the spirit.

We read in Proverbs 18:21 that:

'Death and life are in the power of the tongue.'

Many children have been crushed in their spirits through the harsh words of parents, for their opinions are so important to the child. If they have said words such as: 'You are no good,' 'You're hopeless,' 'You are ugly, no one will want to marry you,' 'You are pathetic,' then the child will believe those words, causing them to go straight into the spirit bringing deep wounding. In this area of words bad news can have the same effect:

'And it shall be that when they say to you, Why do you sigh? that you shall answer, Because of the tidings, When it comes, ... and every spirit will faint.'   (Ezekiel 21:7)

This was true of Jacob's spirit, when he heard the bad tidings concerning his son Joseph:

'I will go down to Sheol (the place of the dead) to my son mourning,'   (Genesis 37:35)

and it was only when the good news came, (that Joseph was still alive) that we are told:

'the spirit of Jacob their father revived (and warmth and life returned).'

Functions Impaired

The function which is impaired when a spirit is crushed is that it becomes unable to comfort, sustain or empower their own, or other people's body and soul. However those with a crushed, bruised and heavy spirit can take courage, for Jesus has promised to restore and revive such people. He describes His role as being:

> *'to send forth as delivered those who are oppressed (who are downtrodden, bruised, crushed, and broken down by calamity).'*
>
> (Luke 4:18b)

Ministering to the Crushed Spirit

The story of Elijah is very helpful here, in the context of ministry, for it gives us a number of clues as to how to help those who are feeling downtrodden on the inside. One of the main lessons we can learn from this story is: be practical! Because the person's own spirit cannot strengthen or comfort their body, they will need to have someone draw alongside them, to do the job for them. God actually sent an angel to bake a cake for Elijah, which is very reminiscent of the time when Jesus provided a breakfast for the weary, crushed disciples (John 20). People who are crushed in spirit do not need another prayer meeting, or Bible study, however good these may be. It would be just one more burden! They need (as Scripture shows) to be loved and shown love, in as many practical ways as possible. The wisdom of God shows that there is a time when cake, bread and fish are more necessary than a portion of the Word.

So look for something that will encourage and comfort the person, depending on the reason and the response to the crushing. For one it may be a holiday, for another a teddy bear, for someone else a favoured pet. One lady whom we ministered to, was so fragile in spirit that the only practical thing that brought her any comfort was to lend her a family dog who took her for long walks! She was able to pour her heart out to the family pet, telling the animal secrets that no other human being knew, or ever needed to know. The walks and the listening ear brought a great deal of strength and comfort to her wounded spirit. If the reason for the crushing of the spirit was a burden too heavy to bear, and it is still present, there may be the need of another person's shoulder, to help bear the burden.

There comes a time, however, when they will need more than the practical. They will need to realise who they are in Christ, and begin to discover or rediscover, the strength which they have in Him. If you do this before the practical, it will have little or no effect. It needs to be done when they are stronger in their body and soul, which is exactly what God did with Elijah. Once he was fed, watered and had slept, God began to challenge him. In response to his cry of self-pity (that he was the only one who hadn't bowed the knee to Baal), God showed him that there were indeed:

> *'7,000 in Israel, all the knees that have not bowed to Baal and every mouth that has not kissed him.'* (1 Kings 18:18)

The person crushed in spirit will need help in renewing their vision. There comes a time when God says to Elijah, 'it is time to move on, I still have a purpose and a vision for you to accomplish.'

As well as being challenged as to who they are in Christ, they will need lots of encouragement and affection. Take plenty of time to feed the Word of God into them, reminding them that God will give them:

> *'the garment (expressive) of praise instead of a heavy, burdened, and failing spirit.'*
> (Isaiah 61:3)

If they are bruised and heavy in their spirits because of authoritarianism, strict leadership, or control, you will need to lift this away from them in prayer, and break, in the name of Jesus, any wrong bondings which may have been formed. For example, one man who came to us for ministry had to be set free from the power and influence of a Brethren leader, under whom he had served for a number of years. Because of the leader's strict legalistic lifestyle and type of control, he had thoroughly crushed this man's spirit and dominated his will. It was only when this bondage was broken that the man moved into a greater measure of freedom and was eventually able to become a leader in another church. This is not to say, however, that this is by any means true of other Brethren leaders, only that it happened in this instance.

As well as breaking any wrong bondings, you will also need to break the power of any harsh or abusive words which may have been spoken. Speak into them the positive in place of the negative. For example: 'You're not hopeless, you are a new creature in Christ Jesus, He loves you and created you for Himself.'

You can then begin to minister healing and deliverance, under the power of the Holy Spirit. He will bring thoughts, words or impressions to your spirit (to that intuitive part), in order that you can minister effectively and enable Him to give them:

> *'the garment (expressive) of praise instead of a heavy, burdened, and failing spirit.'*

> (Isaiah 61:3)

Summary

1. Give **practical** comfort.
2. Build into them a **realisation** of who they are in Christ.
3. Give lots of **encouragement** and **affection**.
4. Help them to renew their **vision**.
5. Feed the **Word of God** into them.

6. Lift off **manipulation** and **control**.
7. Break the power of **words**.
8. Minister **healing** and **deliverance** under the guidance of the Holy Spirit.

Chapter 9

Areas of Damage – A Defiled Spirit

The writer to the Corinthians exhorts:

> *'Let us cleanse ourselves from everything that contaminates and defiles body and spirit.'*
> (2 Corinthians 17:1)

It is not only the body that can become dirty and unclean, but the spirit also. It can pick up dirt, mud and filth, just as surely as the human body. When that happens we cannot communicate with God in the way we were meant to, and because of the filthiness of our spirits we cannot communicate with each other very clearly either. Everything becomes distorted.

The person with a defiled spirit will have a distinct lack of awareness of the presence of God, resulting in difficulty in staying in tune with Him. More likely than not there will be an interference with worship and a desire to run from praise. One lady we were ministering to was virtually unable to stay in the presence of God's people when they were

73

worshipping. She inevitably, 'took to her heels' and ran, unable to bear the Glory of God. The more defilement there is, the harder it will be for the person to stay whilst worship is taking place.

If there is a defilement of spirit there may be an interest in, or a drawing towards, the occult. One young girl of thirteen, brought up in lovely Christian family (although adopted) had, when she became a teenager, a distinct interest in Tarot cards and the Ouija board. We were called in to minister when she was on the point of suicide. The Ouija board kept speaking one word to her continually: 'death'. On investigation we found that her mother had been into the occult and this seemed to have resulted in passing on to the child a generational defilement of spirit. Exodus 20:5 talks about God:

> *'visiting the iniquity of the fathers upon the children to the third and fourth generation of those who hate Me.'*

There may also be a sense of unwholeness in the spirit, especially if there have been any ungodly sexual relationships. (We will look more closely at this area when we consider the causes of a defiled spirit.)

Causes of a Defiled Spirit

One of the prime causes of our spirit becoming dirty or defiled is that each one of us is a sinner and therefore we will pick up dirt, dust or filth on a regular basis. We need to learn to keep a short account with God concerning our sin, continually, in a state of repentance, looking to Him for forgiveness and cleansing. John's letter reminds us that:

> '*If we (freely) admit that we have sinned and confess our sins, He is faithful and just (true to His own nature and promises) and will forgive our sins (dismiss our lawlessness) and (continuously) cleanse us from all unrighteousness.*' (1 John 1:9)

Another cause (as we have seen) is an involvement with the occult, either their own or generational. We have found in a number of instances, that where previous members of the family have been involved in other religions or freemasonry, there is often a confusion in the spirit, thus when reading Scripture the mind may become very confused or sleepy. What is happening? I believe that the defilement of the spirit, due to false worship, has resulted in confusing the mind or the body. Any form of idolatry can, according to Scripture, defile the spirit, as Paul writes to the Corinthians concerning idol worship:

> '*What agreement (can there be between) a temple of God and idols? For we are the temple of the living God: even as God said, I will dwell in and with and among them and will walk in and with and among them, and I will be their God, and they shall be My people. So, come out from among (unbelievers), and separate (sever)*

*yourselves from them, says the Lord, and touch
not (any) unclean thing.'*

(2 Corinthians 6:16, 17)

Luke, in the book of Acts, picks up the same
theme and records that the apostles and the elders
agreed that they should send word to the Gentiles
to:

*'abstain from and avoid anything that has
been polluted by being offered to idols.'*

(Acts 15:20)

Thus we see that contact with any form of idolatry can cause pollution and defilement.

Because sexual intercourse is more than just a
physical act, Paul writes to the Corinthians:

*'do you not know and realize that when a man
joins himself to a prostitute, he becomes one
body with her? The two, it is written, shall
become one flesh.'*

Therefore ungodly or perverted sexual bondings
can be another source of defilement. Whatever is in
the human spirit of one person has the potential of
transferring into the spirit of the other person, thus
defiling them. This is especially true if one of the
partners has been into the occult. According to
Ezekiel prostitution defiles and pollutes. Referring
to prostitution he says:

*'And the Babylonians came to her into the bed of
love, and they defiled her with their evil desire.'*
(Ezekiel 23:17)

Paul urged the Christians to come out from
among unbelievers, because he knew that certain
company can defile the spirit, as do bitter roots.
There is the admonition in Scripture not to let any
bitter root spring up and so defile many (Hebrews
12:15).

Those involved with ministering to others need to
be aware that ministry situations can also cause
defilement and pollution to their spirit. There are a
number of reasons for this: it may be that they enter
ministry without being prepared, or that there is an
area of weakness in their own lives, or maybe are
actively into unconfessed sin themselves. It is very
important that those involved in ministry walk
cleanly before the Lord; learn how to take spiritual
protection and be able to use spiritual hygiene when
necessary. Because people involved with prayer
ministry are usually folk with very sensitive spirits,
it is all too easy for them to become contaminated
by the 'dirt' which they are praying into, if they
forget to prepare their own hearts first.

Functions Impaired

The functions impaired because of a defiled
spirit are: the conscience becomes darkened and it
has difficulty distinguishing between right and
wrong; judgement over sin becomes confused;

communication with God is hindered especially in worship (like interference on radio waves); and the faculties of revelation and intuition are seriously distorted:

> *'Now we are looking in a mirror that gives only a dim (blurred) reflection.'* (1 Corinthians 13:12)

The same principle applies to the human spirit if it is dirty and unclean.

Ministering to the Defiled Spirit

The person needs to be led to a place of repentance concerning any known sin or occult activity which they have been into. If they know of any generational sin they will need to confess it on behalf of their ancestors, just as Ezra (Ezra 9:5–15) and Nehemiah did:

> *'Yes, I and my father's house have sinned,'*
> (Nehemiah 1:6)

asking the Lord to take away the consequences of that sin.

If there have been any ungodly sexual bondings these will need breaking, and the consequences dealt with through prayer. The human spirit will need to be cleansed from any wrongful spirit contamination, remembering that it is the Word of God that cleanses:

'You are cleansed and pruned already, because of the word which I have given you.' (John 15:3)

Throughout the ministry to the person with a defiled spirit, the Holy Spirit will usually bring words of knowledge, wisdom or discernment to the person ministering. It is important to allow Him to take the lead and to remember that, as in every ministry situation, there is no technique, only the Holy Spirit as the leader. Always be aware of the need to look for and deal with the demonic if, and when, necessary.

Summary

1. Lead them to **repantance** for their own, or generational sin.
2. Break any ungodly **bondings**.
3. **Cleanse** the spirit from all defilement.
4. Minister Healing and Deliverance under the guidance of the **Holy Spirit**.

Chapter 10

Areas of Damage –
A Broken Spirit

In the area of being wounded in the human spirit, this is the most serious condition of all. The people who are walking around with a broken spirit are in a very critical condition indeed. Job asserts:

'My Spirit is broken, my days are spent (snuffed out); the grave is ready for me.'   (Job 17:1)

Unfortunately many people assume they are emotionally ill, when really the problem is not in their emotions but in their spirits. This is probably because they feel so sad and grief-stricken, they think it must be emotionally linked. However the sadness and sorrow are primarily the 'cause' of the brokenness in spirit, and not the 'result'. As the writer to Proverbs tells us, the reason for a broken spirit is that:

'By sorrow of heart the spirit is broken.'

I believe that there are more people walking around with a broken spirit who are trying to get healed in their emotions, than we have realised. If the problem is in the spirit, then that is the wound that needs healing. To simply minister into the emotions will only deal with the symptoms and not with the root. However the symptoms do give us a clue as to who may be suffering from this dreadful disease.

What are the symptoms, then, of the one whose spirit is broken? Usually there are a number of physical signs, such as sadness of face. As the writer of Proverbs remarks:

> *'A glad heart makes a cheerful countenance,'*
>
> (Proverbs 15:13)

so conversely, we could conclude that a sad heart makes a sorrowful countenance. This, of course, is borne out by experience (apart from those people who try to put a cheerful face on at all costs) and usually it is very costly! Very often the broken in spirit will show signs of premature ageing: stooped shoulders, greying hair, dragging steps. Why is that? Well according to Proverbs:

> *'A broken spirit dries up the bones.'*
>
> (Proverbs 17:22)

The spirit cannot do its job function of strengthening and empowering the body and soul because of its brokenness, and thus becomes stooped and weary. I walked behind a lady and gentleman last week, who by their whole body appearance and facial expressions, were obviously the recent hearers of bad news. Their broken spirit was so evident to all with the eyes to see. Having prayed with a number of people with arthritis (many of whom have suffered from deep, deep grief way back in their past), the statement in Scripture that a broken spirit dries up the bones is not surprising. That is not to say, however, that **all** arthritis is caused by grief or a broken spirit.

Sleeplessness is another physical symptom:

> *'His (Nebuchadnezzar) spirit was troubled and agitated and his sleep went from him.'*
>
> (Daniel 2:1)

It is not unusual for the broken in spirit to toss and turn most of the night and then fall asleep just as the day dawns. Constant and seemingly inappropriate weeping may be a sign as well, like the lady who had an horrific accident when she was three years old. She would find herself crying for no apparent purpose. One of the reasons, I believe, was that when she was three, alongside bones being broken, her spirit was broken also.

Resorting to anorexic or bulimia type of behaviour can also be a sign of deep grief and a broken spirit.

Another physical manifestation would be the presence of frequent and constantly changing physical infirmities:

> *'The strong spirit of a man sustains him in bodily pain or trouble, but a weak and broken spirit who can raise up or bear?'*
>
> (Proverbs 18:14)

Sometimes people are cruelly labelled as hypochondriacs, when really the physical pain and illnesses are simply the symptoms, the outcome or the result of their broken spirit.

There will also be a number of emotional symptoms, a sense of continual sorrow, sadness, despair and grief or deep and bitter anger leading to a state of rebellion. The person may be, or may become, very dependent and fearful. Often there will be a sense of hopelessness and desolation. Some have described their feelings as **an inner rawness**, a **'bleeding on the inside'** an ache within which gets almost healed, then the pain starts again, like a physical wound with the scab continually being knocked off. Often there is an over-sensitivity, a prickliness about the person. There will probably be an **inability to trust** anyone, for they might hurt you badly again and thus add to your pain. They may have what I would call a 'closed spirit', just as Jacob had, when his sons told him that Joseph was alive:

> *'He (Jacob) refused to be comforted and said, I will go down to Sheol (the place of the dead) to my son mourning. And his father wept for him.'*
>
> (Genesis 37:35)

Very often there will be a deep insecurity and finally a longing for death.

One Christian gentleman (the life and soul of any party) courted his wife from a very early age and was married to her for over forty years. When she died in her sixties, he was so overcome with grief that it caused his spirit to break. This resulted in him grieving himself to death within a very short time.

Causes of a Broken Spirit

The main cause of a broken spirit is that of any loss situation which causes deep sorrow. As we have seen already:

> *'By sorrow of heart the spirit is broken.'*
> (Proverbs 15:13)

Genesis 37:33–35 tells of the deep brokenness of spirit of the patriarch Jacob on hearing of the supposed death of Joseph:

> *'And Jacob tore his clothes, put on sackcloth, and mourned many days for his son.'*
> (Genesis 37:34)

Later in the story we are told:

> *'When he (Jacob) saw the wagons which Joseph had sent to carry him, the spirit of Jacob their father revived.'* (Genesis 45:27)

Thus the loss of people one has loved, either by death, separation or divorce, can break the spirit. However it isn't only the loss of a loved one; the loss of a job or a career can have the same effect, as can the loss of important material things, loss of status or even the removal or loss of a ministry. We prayed with one Pastor who, because he had been betrayed by someone in his fellowship, had eventually lost his congregation. He was absolutely devastated and his spirit was truly broken. We have also ministered to many other Pastors who in their hearts fear failure, and are already beginning to show signs of a fracture in their spirits.

As well as loss or potential loss situations, other causes of a broken spirit would be pre-natal and birth traumas, such as a breech birth, caesarean, or attempted but unsuccessful abortions. If, as we have noted, babies in the womb can pick up in their spirits what is happening in, and around them, then an attempted abortion would surely have a devastating effect. Any present day traumas, such as violent or sudden accidents, acrimonious divorce etc. can also bring deep sorrow and break the spirit.

Rejection at any point is one of the most likely reasons for a person developing a broken spirit and there are a number of 'key times' when this can happen: during any traumatic pre-birth or birth experiences, for example; if a child is conceived in rape or anger, or is the wrong sex at birth, if a child is abandoned by meaningful people, for instance; adopted or fostered children; or those who have lost a parent through death, at an early age; if a child is rejected by their peer group during puberty or their teen years; any life experiences which bring rejection, for example; wives or husbands who have been deserted by their spouses. All of these times and experiences can spell rejection to the inner person and cause a deep brokenness of spirit.

Another cause would be that of betrayal, especially by friends. One lady, who had been recently divorced, said that the cause of her broken spirit was not her husband's unfaithfulness, but the betrayal by her best friend. That was the cut which went the deepest. Any disappointments, unfulfilled dreams or dashed hopes, break the spirit. For example we are told that Hannah was a woman *'of sorrowful spirit'* (1 Samuel 1:15) because of her childlessness. Many women with whom I have prayed and ministered to, because of the barrenness of their wombs, have needed deep ministry into their broken spirits also. These wounds go very deep. If someone gets to a certain age and they feel that life has passed them by, that they will never fulfil their dreams and ambitions, or children leave home against the parents wishes, then hearts may be filled with sadness and sorrow and thus cause the spirit to be broken.

Another major cause of a broken spirit is that of abuse: physical, verbal, emotional or sexual abuse will cause a deep rift in the spirit of the victim, which often leaves the person totally broken on the inside. Having ministered into many, many, people

who have been sexually abused, I am so grateful
that the Lord included this subject in the Scriptures.
There are a number of instances, but I refer to only
one, which is the story of Tamar, who was sexually
abused by her brother Amnon. After he had
raped her, he rejected her, calling his servant and
saying:

> *'Put this women out of my presence now, and
> bolt the door after her.'*   (2 Samuel 13:17)

Later we read that Tamar wandered around:

> *'a desolate women.'*   (2 Samuel 13:20)

She was totally broken in spirit, as we can see
from that very descriptive word, 'desolation', which
means solitary, uninhabited, ruinous, neglected,
barren, forlorn, disconsolate and wretched.

Functions Impaired

The function which is most damaged here is the
almost total breakdown of communication. Because
the spirit is broken it cannot feed life, strength,
encouragement or comfort to the person concerned,
or to anyone else. It has difficulty communicating
with God or receiving from the Holy Spirit in the
whole area of the intuition or the conscience. Thus
the broken in spirit behaves like a broken car, with
all primary and secondary functions seriously
malfunctioning!

Ministering to the Broken Spirit

First of all the deep wounds need to be acknow-
ledged, both by the one ministering and by the
person themselves. It is much easier, and more
common, to do this if a person has a physical
wound, but those with a wounded, broken spirit,
need sympathy and acknowledgement also. Sometimes the recognition of the problem and the source
of the pain is in itself a major step towards healing.
As with any physical wound, there will need to be a
time of probing and cleansing. Most sufferers will
find this a very difficult process and will want to
postpone or delay the 'operation' for as long as possible. Gently, but firmly, they will need to be
brought to face the issues and the cause of the
brokenness. They need to see that for true and lasting healing to take place, the wound needs to be
exposed. It is vitally important that the person
ministering be like a qualified surgeon, digging
gently but deeply into the wound, continually
exposing it to the Holy Spirit. The reason for the
probing is in order that any infections which are
there may be taken out of the wound and we
are not therefore guilty of the accusation that:

> *'They have healed the wound of the daughter of
> My people only lightly and slightingly, saying,
> Peace, peace, when there is no peace.'*
> (Jeremiah 8:11)

The infections will vary tremendously, depending

on the reason for the wounding. As you wield the knife, under the direction of the Holy Spirit, you may find hardness of heart, resentment, deep anger, bitterness and unforgiveness. Very often during ministry, people will say such words as: 'Why did God let that happen to me?' 'If He is so good, how come this awful thing happened?' 'Why did my marriage fail? We both prayed and loved the Lord.' 'Why have my children gone off the rails?' The words need to be spoken out and the bitterness behind them recognised and released.

When all the infections have been drained away at the Cross, then there will probably be many forgiveness issues to deal with. There will be some people they will need to forgive, including many in the Body of Christ who have walked past their pain because it was on the inside. They may even be holding a grudge against God Himself, if they feel that He has been the cause of their sorrow. Of course with our minds we know God is not guilty, but if the person feels it in their spirit, then they need to choose to forgive even the Lord Himself. One of the key people they will need to express forgiveness towards will be themselves, for many of them will feel guilty for 'not being stronger', 'for not coping better' etc.

Bitter roots need to be confronted and removed. Many of these will be linked with inner vows which they have made at the time of the wounding. 'I will never give myself to a person again', 'I have failed', 'I am useless', 'God cannot possibly use me again'.

Such bitter roots need exposing and removing through the power of the Holy Spirit.

The person needs to be encouraged to turn from their own solutions, which may have been many and varied: sexual satisfaction as with the woman at the well (John 4); the desire for retaliation; a wanting to get revenge for the hurt and pain which eats away on the inside; a craving for food and comfort eating; a desire for new clothes in order to try and develop a new image and hopefully a new lifestyle; the use of escape mechanisms, such as sport or television taken to excess; becoming a workaholic in order to mask the pain or turning to drugs and alcohol. Some people develop a 'Back to the wall' syndrome (no one is going to hurt me again), or even use other people as a solution, and dependence may then become an issue.

Once the infections, bitter roots, and the person's own solutions have been exposed and dealt with, then we need to look for and minister into the roots and causes of the wounding. This can only be done effectively under the guidance and gifting of the Holy Spirit. If you have a car that is totally broken down, you send for the best mechanic possible to mend it. If you can get the original creator, so much the better. As we have seen, it is God Himself who formed the spirit of man within him (Zechariah 12:1), and it is the Holy Spirit who brings that spirit to life, when it is dead in trespasses and sin (John 6:63). Therefore it would make sense to call upon Him when the spirit needs fixing and healing. Jesus

Himself affirms at the beginning of His ministry that He was anointed to:

> *'preach the good news (the Gospel) to the poor; He has sent Me to announce release to the captives and recovery of sight to the blind, to send forth as delivered those who are oppressed (who are downtrodden, bruised, crushed, and broken down by calamity).'* (Luke 4:18)

So we see that Father, Son and Holy Spirit are involved in the creation and healing of the human spirit, which is why we need Him to be present whenever we are ministering into this area.

Once the roots of the brokenness have been exposed and dealt with (either by inner healing prayers, deliverance or both) then the person will need lots of after-care and affection. There is a real need for godly people, at this point of ministry, who will take time to build up and strengthen those who are recuperating, feeding the truth of God into them, the truth that they are special, that there is hope, that God still has a purpose for them. They will need lots of tender expressions of love from the Body of Christ, a pouring into them of the *'balm of Gilead'*, a deep acceptance of them as people on the road to healing.

Summary

1.   An **acknowledgement** of the wound.
2.   **Infections** to be removed from the wound.

3. A **cleansing** of the wound.
4. A turning from their own **solutions**.
5. A need to uncover the **roots**.
6. Minister under the guidance of the **Holy Spirit**.
7. Feed in encouragement, love and acceptance.

Conclusion

Only Jesus can heal the broken hearted. That's His job description, but as part of the Body of Christ, it's also yours! Those who are called to minister healing in the name of Jesus need to recognize that some people for whom they pray will be wounded not only in their bodies and souls but also in their human spirits. We pray with Paul that those we meet in the Body of Christ will become sound in: *'spirit and soul and body'* (1 Thessalonians 5:23) and in order for that to happen, we need to learn how to co-operate with the Holy Spirit, in order that they may become whole.

One of the most beautiful qualities of the Holy Spirit is the one which I mentioned previously, concerning His ability to draw alongside the one with a wounded spirit, and align Himself with them. Thus the Holy Spirit and the human spirit become engaged like cogs in a wheel. When this happens, He does for the timid, the imprisoned, the defiled, the crushed and the broken, what they cannot do for themselves. He Himself performs and undergirds the job functions of the human spirit until eventually the person comes to a place of wholeness and healing. This is the meaning of the title *'Paracletos'*.

Do you remember what His and the human spirit's job functions are? To **communicate** life; to **comfort** those who mourn; to bring **strength** to the weak; to **reveal** the Father's heart; to bring **conviction** of sin; to take part in **creative** activities; to bring **hope** to the hopeless; to pour **affection** on the affectionless; to grant **security** to the fearful; to bring **release** to the imprisoned; to **revive** the fainting and to enable God's plans to be brought to fruition, thus bringing in the Kingdom of God.

To be a part of the ministry to the wounded human spirit is a tremendous responsibility, but it is also a wonderful privilege.

Deeper Healing for the Human Spirit

Contents

Preface

I have written this book for two groups of readers: first for those who are involved in Prayer Ministry and who want to know more about how to pray healing into the human spirit. Secondly, for those who have expressed their interest in how the condition of our human spirit has an impact upon our soul and our bodies and thus on our physical well-being.

According to Hebrews 4:12,

> '... *the word of God is living and powerful, and sharper than any two-edged sword, piercing even to the division of soul and spirit, and of joints and marrow, and is a discerner of the thoughts and intents of the heart.*'

Thus, we see that according to the New Testament man is a tripartite being: spirit, soul and body, and it is obvious that each part must of necessity interact and have an impact on the other parts. We have recognised for many years the influence of the mind (the soul area) upon the body. We call these psychosomatic diseases: 'mind over matter'.

Most people are also aware that if we are physically ill this will affect the spirit and the soul. For example, when our bodies are suffering we can easily become 'low in spirit', be 'cast down' or become 'mentally confused'. It is also true that if we are damaged in our emotions, then this will have an effect on how we feel physically, spiritually and mentally.

One of the areas which we have been researching is the important role that the human spirit plays in the matter of our well being, and whether a wounded spirit could have a detrimental impact upon our souls and our bodies. (For more information on how the human spirit can be wounded, please refer to our book *Healing the Human Spirit*.)[1] It was because of our study for writing that book that certain questions arose:

- *Does the state of my human spirit have an impact upon my body and soul?*
- *Is it possible for my physical well-being to be dependent, to some extent, on the health of my spirit?*

(It would probably be helpful, for the reader, to study this present book in the light of *Healing the Human Spirit*.)

As we have travelled and shared our research, people have asked if the answers to these and other questions could be available to them in written form. This small book is the result, and we offer it to you as a foundation for your own thoughts and deliberations. Please take it as an **exploration** of the subject rather than a finished article. We are still in the process of learning and simply share our thoughts with you. The way in which the human spirit affects the soul and the body is a very important subject, and one which deserves and needs much thought.

[1]   Ruth Hawkey, *Healing the Human Spirit*, New Wine Press, 1996.

We want to emphasise strongly however, at the beginning of this book, that the condition of the human spirit is **only one of a number of reasons for sickness** in the soul and the body. There are many more (universal sin, poverty, poor housing, Satan etc.) which it is not our remit to consider.

Ruth Hawkey

Chapter 1

God's Heart Is for Health

'Bless the LORD, O my soul;
And forget not all His benefits:
Who forgives all your iniquities,
Who heals all your diseases.'
(Psalm 103:2–3)

According to the Scriptures, man was created sinless and healthy. We are told that:

'God saw everything that He had made, and indeed it was very good.'   (Genesis 1:31)

Until sin entered the world, Adam walked in perfect health. The breath of life had been breathed into him by God,

'And the LORD God formed man of the dust of the ground, and breathed into his nostrils the breath of life; and man became a living being.'   (Genesis 2:7)

This breath of life was daily replenished as he was allowed to eat freely of the tree of life.

The godly order of man's creation was that God 'formed' Adam's body out of the dust and that his soul, his *nephesh*, came into being when God 'breathed' into him the breath of life. Thus, it would appear that if we consider man to be a tripartite being, then Adam's spirit, the breath of life, which came direct from God, is of a higher order than his body and his soul. This would in God's plan allow Adam to be led by his human spirit, under the direction of the Holy Spirit, his human spirit providing a covering and a protection for his body and soul.

I am aware that some argue that there was no trichotomy in Hebrew psychology, no triple division of human personality into 'body, soul, and spirit', and that an exhaustive description of human personality was given by saying 'body and soul'. However, it is recognised that although in early Hebrew thinking 'soul and spirit' might denote the same thing, nevertheless because 'spirit' originated from God as a divine energy, it 'naturally suggests a higher conception of the life of man, as drawn from God'.[2]

Mary, the mother of Jesus, a Hebrew of the Hebrews, recognised the truth of this. In her song of adoration she distinguishes between the soul and the spirit:

> *'And Mary said:*
> *"My soul* [psyche] *magnifies the Lord,*
> *And my spirit* [pneuma] *has rejoiced in*
> *God my Saviour." '*　　　　　　(Luke 1:46–47)

God's heart is that humanity should enjoy good health in his spirit, soul and body. However, whilst that is in God's heart, there is no denying the fact that very often the opposite appears to be true. Disease and ill-health

---

[2] 'Hebrew Psychology', H. Wheeler Robinson in *The People and the Book*, A.S. Peake (ed.), Oxford University Press.

abound. Sicknesses and viruses seem to be everywhere, and increasing.

Man's Sinfulness

As we have already stated, it is very important to emphasise that there are **many reasons for pain and suffering**, some of which are social, some physical, some (according to the story of Job) sent by Satan and some that are beyond our understanding. Nevertheless, many people believe that disobedience to God's commandments is one of the underlying causes of much of the disease within our world. It is interesting to note that, according to the Scriptures, it was because of man's disobedience to God's law that sickness and disease first entered the human race.

> *'And the* Lord *God commanded the man, saying, "Of every tree of the garden you may freely eat; but of the tree of the knowledge of good and evil you shall not eat, for in the day that you eat of it you shall surely die."'*
> (Genesis 2:16–17)

When Adam disobeyed the above commandment God's order was reversed. The soul and the body took control and the human spirit took a subordinate position. We see evidence of this in the fact that when Adam and Eve sinned, their eyes were opened and they realised that they were naked. Before they sinned they were, I believe, in such perfect spirit-to-Spirit communion with God, that they were clothed in the brightness of the glory of God. They walked and talked, spirit to Spirit, with their Creator. Nakedness was not a term in their vocabulary! It was only after they had sinned that they lost their glorious covering, which I believe was the covering of the human spirit, under the covering of the Holy Spirit. Genesis chapter 3 records:

> *'And they heard the sound of the LORD God walking in the garden in the cool of the day, and Adam and his wife hid themselves from the presence of the LORD God among the trees of the garden. Then the LORD God called to Adam and said to him, "Where are you?" So he said, "I heard Your voice in the garden, and I was afraid because I was naked; and I hid myself."'* (Genesis 3:8–10)

Moses on the mountaintop experienced, for a brief period, the same glorious radiance,

> *'Now it was so, when Moses came down from Mount Sinai (and the two tablets of the Testimony were in Moses' hand when he came down from the mountain), that Moses did not know that the skin of his face shone while he talked with Him.'* (Exodus 34:29)

Before Jesus came to the earth, He fully experienced this glorious radiance because He was one with the Father, but as the hymn writer says 'He laid His glory by, He wrapped Him in our clay.' However, on the mount of transfiguration the disciples for a brief moment saw His glory:

> *'... He was transfigured before them. His face shone like the sun, and His clothes became as white as the light.'* (Matthew 17:2)

When Adam disobeyed God's commandment, he reaped the consequences; he died spiritually and eventually physically; he lost the covering of glory; he was no longer a spiritual man (*pneumatikos* – of the spirit). Instead he became a carnal man (*sarkikos* – of the body) or a natural man (*psychikos* – belonging to the soul). God excluded him from the Garden of Eden and from being able to eat of the tree of life and live forever.

Thus, we see that when man sinned he introduced into the human race a deadly virus, which, whilst it will eventually cause death, also causes havoc with man's health along the way. Sometimes it is personal sin and disobedience, which brings disease and ultimately death, and sometimes it is corporate sin and disobedience.

The Power of the Cross

God, however, did not leave man in his sin or his sickness. We read in the Scriptures that:

> [God said], *"If you diligently heed the voice of the LORD your God and do what is right in His sight, give ear to His commandments and keep all His statutes, I will put none of the diseases on you which I have brought on the Egyptians. For I am the LORD who heals you."'*
>
> (Exodus 15:26)

One of the names attributed to God in the Old Testament is the name 'Jehovah Rapha' ('raw-faw'); it can mean 'to mend' (by stitching), i.e. (figuratively) 'to cure'. It is interesting to note that when Adam and Eve sinned the Lord stitched clothes for them! He covered the immediate consequences of their sin, which was deep shame and fear, by providing another covering for them. He then sent them on their way out of the Garden.

Many people believe that the context of the phrase *'I am the LORD who heals you'* alludes to the future healing which flows to us from the cross.

> *'Now when they came to Marah, they could not drink the waters of Marah, for they were bitter. Therefore, the name of it was called Marah. And the people complained against Moses, saying, "What shall we drink?" So he cried out to the LORD, and the LORD showed him a tree. When he cast it into the waters, the waters were made sweet.'* (Exodus 15:23–25)

Sin and sickness are primarily the result of man's disobedience, and Jesus dealt with both of them at the cross by the shedding of His precious blood. He was a man who was totally obedient to God's commandments being: *'obedient to the point of death, even the death of the cross'* (Philippians 2:8). As such, He broke the pattern of man's sin. He fully obeyed the first commandment and added the second, emphasising that it is also important to love our neighbours as ourselves:

> *'Jesus said to him, "'You shall love the LORD your God with all your heart, with all your soul, and with all your mind.' This is the first and great commandment. And the second is like it: 'You shall love your neighbour as yourself.' On these two commandments hang all the Law and the Prophets."'* (Matthew 22:37–40)

Obedience – a Key to Health

Jesus walked with God; was filled with the Holy Spirit; was obedient to God and was a man whose spirit was whole and who walked in perfect health. Thus, we see that on consideration of the Scriptures, there certainly seems to be a definite relationship between keeping God's commandments, which is an activity of the spirit, and the enjoyment of physical health. Will you note that it is important to love God, others and ourselves in order to be healthy? Some of us find it easier to love God and other people than it is to love ourselves. It is in this area that we maybe need to do the most work.

A Healthy Spirit

I would suggest to you that in the same way as the obedience of Jesus to God's laws brought health to Him, so our obedience to God's commandments is an important factor in enabling health to flow to us. That is not to say, by any means, that it is the only factor. As we have already stated, there are many other reasons for a person to become physically ill. I would, however, propose to you that a person's physical, emotional, mental and volitional health flows from a healthy spirit, which is in loving communion with God. However, at the risk of unnecessarily repeating myself, let me assert yet again that this does **not** mean that a holy person does not get ill, for as we have already stated a number of times, there are many other reasons for disease. We are simply considering the proposition that a wounded human spirit is one of them.

In the light of the example of Jesus, we feel that it is relevant to ask the following question: *'What exactly does it mean to have a healthy spirit?'* I would like to suggest the following answer. A healthy spirit is one that:

- is obedient to God's commands
- is under the control of the Holy Spirit

- has control over the soul and the body (godly order)
- functions as God intended

Let us look at the functions of the human spirit (these are discussed more fully in *Healing the Human Spirit*).[3] Briefly, they are as follows:

- To communicate life to the soul and the body[4]
- To communicate comfort and strength to the soul and the body
- To empower and to strengthen the soul and the body
- To communicate truth to the soul and the body
- To convict through the conscience
- To be creative
- To facilitate God's work

Summary

1. The breaking of God's commandments is a sin and according to Scripture, sin (either personal or corporate) or the result of sin, can cause disease.
2. Obedience to God's commandments is essential to healthy living.
3. We can only fully obey God's commandments when our human spirit is healthy and functioning as God intended.

In the light of the above there are a number of areas which we need to consider:

[3] Ruth Hawkey, *Healing the Human Spirit*, New Wine Press, 1996.
[4] For more exploration as to how 'life' is fed to the soul and the body please refer to the Appendix.

1. Does Scripture support the view that there is an *interaction* between the human spirit, soul and the body, either for good or ill?
2. If a person has a *wounded spirit* could that allow, enable or cause disease in the soul and the body?
3. Does Scripture support the view that *sinful attitudes* can cause disease in the body?
4. Could the health of my spirit *affect* the health of someone to whom I am closely bonded, or conversely could their spirit affect mine?
5. Is it the job of the *human spirit* to help the soul and the body when they become ill?
7. Are there any *keys to healthy living*?

Whilst it is an undoubted fact that disease attacks a person from many angles, I believe that the answers to all of the above questions are a definite 'yes' and in the following chapters we will consider each of them in turn.

Chapter 2

Scriptural Evidence

'For the word of God is living and powerful,
and sharper than any two-edged sword,
piercing even to the division of soul and spirit,
and of joints and marrow.'
(Hebrews 4:12)

The first question we need to consider is this: 'Does Scripture support the view that there is an ***interaction*** between the human spirit, the soul and the body, either for good or for ill?' We are told in the Bible that,

> '... *the word of God is living and powerful, and sharper than any two-edged sword, piercing even to the division of soul and spirit, and of joints and marrow, and is a discerner of the thoughts and intents of the heart.'*
> (Hebrews 4:12)

Thus we see that man is so closely joined in his spirit, soul and body that only the Word of God can separate them.

According to W.E. Vine, the language of Hebrews 4:12 'suggests the extreme difficulty of distinguishing between the soul and the spirit, alike in their nature and in their activities. Generally speaking the spirit is the higher, the soul the lower element. The spirit may be recognised as the life principle bestowed on man by God, the soul as the resulting life constituted in the individual, the body being the material organism animated by soul and spirit'.[5]

I would like to show you some evidence from the Scriptures that there is a definite interaction between the spirit, the soul and the body in the area of health. For example, let us look at the woman who Jesus healed on the Sabbath day.

> *'Now He was teaching in one of the synagogues on the Sabbath. And behold, there was a woman who had a spirit of infirmity eighteen years, and was bent over and could in no way raise herself up.'* (Luke 13:10–11)

What caused her body to be bent? Jesus says that it was *'a spirit of infirmity'*. The interesting point here is that a spirit (either evil or human) has had an influence upon the woman's body, and no matter how hard she tried, she could not raise herself up. The spirit is keeping the body and the soul under its control. (The enemy often imitates the godly order.) Her body and her soul were not able to overcome the physical incapacity from which she was suffering.

In the story of Daniel, we find that the soul area has a definite impact upon the human spirit. The visions, which he had in his head (mind), had an influence upon his spirit and caused it to be grieved, for he says,

> *'I, Daniel, was grieved in my spirit within my body, and the visions of my head troubled me.'* (Daniel 7:15)

[5] W.E. Vine, *Expository Dictionary*, Oliphants.

We see the same influence recorded in Daniel chapter 5. Here we see that the king's thoughts (his soul area), cause such a reaction within his body that his hips become painful, and cause a reaction in his knees.

> *'Then the king's countenance changed and his thoughts troubled him, so that the joints of his hips were loosened and his knees knocked against each other.'*
>
> (Daniel 5:6)

Meanwhile Daniel had another vision, which resulted in making him sick in his body,

> *'And I, Daniel, fainted and was sick for days; afterward I arose and went about the king's business. I was astonished by the vision, but no one understood it.'*
>
> (Daniel 8:27)

Jezebel recognised this interaction of spirit, soul and body. When she looked at Ahab's face and demeanour she understood that he was sulking and rebellious in his spirit. This caused him to have no appetite for food:

> *'Jezebel his wife came to him, and said to him, "Why is your spirit so sullen that you eat no food?"'*
>
> (1 Kings 21:5)

We see the same interaction in the story of Hannah, a woman who had a *'sorrowful spirit'* because she was childless. This sadness in her spirit put her off her food and her sleep and caused constant weeping. We would probably say today that she was suffering from deep depression.

Jesus suffered such agonies of spirit in the garden of Gethsemane that it caused an amazing physical reaction. He began to sweat great drops of blood:

> *'And being in agony, He prayed more earnestly. Then His sweat became like great drops of blood falling down to the ground.'* (Luke 22:44)

Sweating is the body's response to try to regulate the temperature when under emotional pressure, caused in this instance by the agony in His spirit. Evidently traumatic events, which affect the spirit, can have an impact upon the soul and the body.

Let me give you a recent illustration that a friend shared with me. A man interred in a concentration camp during the Second World War suffered such agonies of spirit and soul that for years he was unable to share his painful memories. He had, however, a small case in which he placed all of his belongings from that painful time and which he kept locked. No one in the family ever looked into the case and he never opened it himself. As well as keeping the case firmly locked, he kept his emotions locked up too. The family were never able to get him to express his pain or his memories from that time. His human spirit was crushed through that traumatic experience. It could not comfort and sustain his soul, and his emotions and his body bore the consequences. When he went into hospital, very ill and elderly, he insisted that his small precious case went too. It was only when he died that the family looked in the case to find that it contained a meagre record of his time in the camp: a pitiful shirt, a diary of events and one or two other painful but precious memorabilia.

The following story also illustrates how a distressing event can have an impact upon the human spirit, which then goes on to cause physical and emotional turmoil. An officer in the military, who during the war went to visit Belsen concentration camp, was so severely traumatised at the sight of the mutilated bodies, the bones and the carnage, that he was completely devastated. From that moment on he suffered dreadfully physically, emotionally and mentally. In old age he went into hospital for treatment because he was very ill, very yellow and very thin; in fact, the doctors described his condition as 'skin and bones'. They said his illness was 'Belsen Jaundice'. It was as though what he had felt and seen in his spirit eventually had an outworking in his body.

Chapter 3

A Wounded Spirit

'My spirit is broken,
My days are extinguished.'
(Job 17:1)

We will now consider the second question that we posed earlier: 'If a person has a **wounded spirit**, will that allow, enable or cause disease in the soul and the body?' In the light of the words from Proverbs it would certainly seem to be true:

'... a broken spirit dries the bones.' (Proverbs 17:22b)

When sin entered the world, man's spirit, as well as rebelling against the laws of God, stopped functioning in the way in which God had intended. His purpose was that the human spirit would be in control of the soul and the body under the direction of the Holy Spirit, feeding life, strength, encouragement, comfort and revelation into the person. If the human spirit is damaged then this doesn't happen as God planned.

The following chapter, 'An Orphan and a Starved Spirit', will be illustrative of the kind of wounding which can take place in the human spirit and the possible consequences. When damage to the spirit occurs the soul and the body lack the direction and the support of the human spirit and may

119

become open to disease and sickness. Our spirit may be so wounded or defiled that it tells lies to the person, i.e. that they are unlovely, unworthy, guilty, etc. Therefore, instead of feeding love and acceptance into the soul and the body, it feeds the opposite and this may open us up to ill health.

Depending upon the wounding of the spirit certain diseases may take root. For example:

▶ *A timid spirit*

A person who has a **timid spirit** (2 Timothy 1:7) will be unable to comfort, empower or strengthen the soul and the body, and so certain fears and phobias may grow in their mind. On the other hand their body may reflect what is happening in their spirit. For example, one young man who suffered from severe back pain due to a car accident continued to walk with a stoop even when the pain had lifted. (He had had much prayer and often the pain would ease for a number of days and then eventually return.) There could be a number of reasons for this: the continual stooping may have been because his body had simply become used to walking slightly bent, or it may have been that at the time of the accident, his human spirit felt the blow as well as his body. This would have the potential of causing a timid spirit, and for complete healing to take place he would need to have prayer into his human spirit as well as for his body. He is at present in the process of healing.

As a young five-year-old Betty was often left at home when her parents had to go out early to open the baker's shop which they owned. It was only for a short while and everything was considered safe and secure. It was during the Second World War. One day the sirens sounded and Betty began to panic! It had never happened before and she desperately ran from room to room searching for her mother, until she eventually tried to get out of the front door, which had been locked by her mother for Betty's safety.

Meanwhile her mother had dashed up the street from the shop and was frantically trying to get into the house. Betty was so terrified that she 'couldn't think straight'. Her thoughts were scrambled. From the moment she started school she suffered from dyslexia. As an adult she received prayer into her timidity of spirit. She testifies that as prayer was said for her, she felt as though a blanket fell over and around her and a deep peace settled within her. The next morning she was able to read aloud a passage from the Scriptures to a group of people. Normally she would have had to practise it continually before doing so, but that morning she found that her dyslexia had been healed. It was as though when peace settled on her timid, frightened, panicky spirit, the outworking in her body was the healing of her dyslexia.

▶ *An imprisoned spirit*

A person who has an **imprisoned spirit** (Psalm 143:3b) will be unable to communicate life to the soul and the body. In fact, it may feed a sense of bondage into the soul and the body resulting in addictive behaviour. A lady who works with young people who are addicted to drugs wonders if the terrible traumas which many of them seem to have experienced in their childhood could have caused bondage in their spirits, resulting in them becoming physically bound in their bodies to drink and drugs, etc.

▶ *A defiled spirit*

A person who has a **defiled spirit** (2 Corinthians 7:1) will have a conscience that is hardened to sin and this may feed deception into the soul and the body. If a person's spirit has been defiled then it will not be able to distinguish between what is good and what is evil and, as we will see in chapter 5, sinful attitudes and actions may be the result. This can, of course, result in physical disease. The function of the conscience will be impaired and will not be able to guide the soul (the will) to make right choices. This may lead to a lifestyle that could bring disease upon the person. For example, ungodly sex may lead to sexually transmitted diseases. A person may become addicted to certain substances or behaviour etc.

Many other situations can defile the spirit. We heard of a man who went to Rwanda on a recent work visit and was taken to a genocide site in a school. This was a place which the government had encouraged people to go to, in order to be safe from marauding gangs. About 50,000 people had taken their advice. Unfortunately the place which they were told would be safe was not. The militia came and murdered them. It was a tragic spot, made more so by the fact that a large number of bodies had been left in the school. They had been painted with lime and this man, along with others, was encouraged to take photographs. He felt defiled in his spirit. One could imagine the physical stress and disease, which could have followed such tragic scenes. It is important to emphasise that not all memorials are like this one. Many are respectful of the dead, and leave the spirit touched but not necessarily open to defilement.

▶ *A crushed spirit*
A person who has a **crushed spirit** (Psalm 34:18) will be unable to comfort and sustain the soul and the body, and may feed into the person a deep sense of despair instead. For

example, one person who was crushed by his fellowship felt for many months a deep sense of weariness in his bones and tremendous muscle pain. He dragged himself around, with little enjoyment of life. His testimony is that when his spirit was healed his physical health improved tremendously.

▶ *A broken spirit*

A person who has a **broken spirit** (Job 17:1) will be unable to feed life, strength, encouragement, or comfort to themselves. In fact, they have no ability to nourish themselves and therefore may be open to sickness and disease. One woman in Canada, who was broken in her spirit, could not get up in the mornings she felt so weak. Her marriage had broken down and the result was that she was drained emotionally, she had no physical strength, and before long she became physically ill. Fortunately her friends prayed for her daily and fed the Word of God into her. They had discerned that it was primarily a 'human spirit' problem rather than a 'physical' problem. When her spirit was strengthened, she became emotionally and physically strong.

▶ *An orphan spirit*

A person who has an **orphan spirit** (Psalm 27:10) will have little ability to communicate life, strength, or comfort to the soul and the body. Instead, it may feed a deep sense of loneliness and isolation into the person resulting in depression and despair. One woman who was deeply rejected by her mother as a child couldn't receive or retain love, comfort or acceptance by her family as an adult. Her husband would endeavour to assure her of his love but all his protestations would be turned aside by her words, 'Oh you are just saying that.' For many years she suffered from deep depression and it was only when she had prayer into a 'lost child' that she began to move into healing.

▶ *A starved spirit*

A person who has a **starved spirit** (Psalm 142:3) will be unable to communicate life to the soul and the body. It will be unable to comfort the individual and may feed self-rejection into them instead. One woman, who was married to a service man in Germany, was secretary to a local parish priest. She became a 'born-again Christian' and the priest rejected her testimony and her experience. Shortly after this she moved to Scotland and linked up with other Christians. By this time she was very anorexic. She gradually got worse and the local pastor called her church to pray and fast for her. One day a lovely Christian woman read in her Bible, *'the master cursed the servant'*, and she felt that this was a word for the woman they were praying for. She shared it with the prayer group, and they prayed and broke any words of curse that may have been spoken over her by the parish priest. From that moment she began to recover, and now she is the mother of two lovely children. The word of the Lord set her free. It was as though the parish priest rejected her spiritual experience, and this rejection had starved and wounded her human spirit. Before long the starvation in her spirit became a physical starvation and she began to suffer from anorexia.

The soul that is not loved by the spirit (love yourself), may look in inappropriate places for love, comfort and strength which could lead to disease in the body. Instead of affirmation being fed into the soul and the body from the spirit, self-rejection may flow and lead to disease in the soul and the body. If the spirit cannot be creative what will this do to the soul and the body? It will surely become frustrated and anxious, having no outlet for those godly expressions of joy. There will be little nurturing or strengthening of the soul and the body, and these may then go on to become weak and diseased. We will consider in more detail the consequences of a wounded spirit upon the soul (especially the emotional area) in chapter 6.

Henry Wright, a Pastor who is much used in the healing ministry, has written in his book, *A More Excellent Way*[6] that about seventy to eighty per cent of all diseases considered incurable have a spiritual root. The psychiatrist William Sadler says that:

'The majority of people liberally feed their bodies and make generous provision for their mental nourishment. But the vast majority pay little attention to their spiritual nutrition and as a result the spiritual nature is so weakened that it is unable to exercise the restraining influence over the mind, which would enable it to surmount its difficulties and maintain an atmosphere above conflict and despondency.'[7]

---

6   Pastor Henry Wright, *A More Excellent Way*, Pleasant Valley Publications.
7   William Sadler, *Practice of Psychiatry*, St Louis, C.V. Mosby Co., 1953.

Chapter 4

An Orphan and a Starved Spirit

'The helpless commits himself to You;
You are the helper of the fatherless.'
(Psalm 10:14)

An Orphan Spirit

A person with an **orphan spirit** is one who is not necessarily an 'orphan' in reality, but someone who feels an 'orphan' on the inside, i.e. in the inner man. In our experience this is not as rare a condition as many people would think. We have prayed for a number of people like this, people who stumble through life feeling lost and lonely on the inside. The psalmist sums up the depth of the pain:

'For I am poor and needy,
And my heart is wounded within me.' (Psalm 109:22)

Causes of an Orphan Spirit

The overriding reason for a person to be orphaned in their human spirit is a lack of close bonding at a very early age. There are many reasons for this lack of bonding, one of which is that the child perceives rejection within the womb. One lady who gave birth to a still-born child hardened her heart at the next pregnancy. This was a natural defence mechanism in order to protect herself from further possible pain. However, the child in the womb felt deep rejection in her spirit and when she was born she turned away from the mother, refusing to bond with her. It is the testimony of her parents that from the very beginning the child was always as 'stiff as a piece of cardboard' if they tried to touch her or pick her up. We prayed for the daughter, into the time when she was in the womb, asking the Lord to lift away 'perceived rejection' and to form a godly bonding with her parents. She then worked with the Lord to establish healthy relationships with them.

If a child has been conceived in rape or anger, there is a very strong possibility that the mother will reject the baby whilst it is in the womb and it is likely that the baby will then go on to reject the parents at birth. Sometimes a parent will refuse to bond with the baby for other reasons: for example if the baby is going to be put up for adoption or if the parent and child are separated immediately after birth. This may be because the mother or the baby is seriously ill. One lady who we prayed for was put into an incubator for several days and because of difficult circumstances was only visited by nurses and doctors at set times. It was many days before she was reunited with her mother, by which time the 'loneliness' of spirit had taken root. It took many sessions of prayer ministry into her spirit to bring her to a place of acceptance of herself and a willingness to trust other people.

Such people will find it very difficult to bond with Father God. They long to have a deeper relationship with Him, but it is mainly head knowledge and not heart knowledge. In fact they find it difficult to form and maintain any long-lasting relationships. If they do manage to sustain one they will be continually testing the other person: 'If I do this, will you still love me?'

The person who is orphaned on the inside will find it very difficult to give love and yet they will be longing to receive it. They will probably stiffen up if you approach them, because they are frightened of love. They will find 'the offering of the peace' in a church service very difficult and they will not be able to hug other people freely. A person with an orphan spirit often continually searches for a mother or a father figure. They have deep wounds in their spirit and they are always on the lookout for someone to fill that gap.

Another reason for an orphan spirit is when a child is separated from his or her parents at a key time in their life. For example if a parent dies when a child is at a very vulnerable age or maybe one of the parents suddenly disappears out of their life due to an acrimonious divorce. We have found that some people have developed an orphan spirit due to being sent to a boarding school at a particularly vulnerable age. On the other hand some children thrive on that experience.

Functions Impaired

A person who has an orphaned spirit will find **communication** with God and with other people very difficult indeed. Because they have never known the comfort, the deep comfort, of 'belonging' they will find it almost impossible to **comfort** others or themselves.

Ministering to the Orphan Spirit

It is very important to be very sensitive to the deep pain of the wounds within the person with an orphan spirit. There will be a need to build up trust with the person and this may take a little time. We will consider some keys to prayer ministry into the human spirit in a later chapter but I include here some basic guidelines:

- Look for the reason for the wounding. It is always important to understand 'why' the person has become damaged in their spirit, in order for you to pray specifically. Words of knowledge from the Holy Spirit will be very helpful here.
- Teach into the Father-heart of God.
- Ask the Holy Spirit to bring into being a godly bonding with the Heavenly Father. He is a creator.
- Minister to the orphan through the love of the Father speaking deep into their spirit, 'you're not an orphan; the Father loves you; He put you together inside your mother's womb.'
- Use the Word of God as you speak into their spirit:

> *'The helpless commits himself to You;*
> *You are the helper of the fatherless.'* (Psalm 10:14)

> *'A father of the fatherless, a defender of*
> *   widows,*
> *Is God in His holy habitation.*
> *God sets the solitary in families;*
> *He brings out those who are bound*
> *   into prosperity.'* (Psalm 68:5–6)

- Encourage them to lay aside any habits and behaviour patterns which they have developed as a result of the wounding within.

A person with an orphan spirit will need much love, nurture and kind 're-parenting'. A church with spiritual mothers and fathers are a godsend to those people who are orphaned on the inside, for good parenting is a major part of their healing.

A Starved Spirit

Some people do not live their lives with the fullness of joy and vitality that God intended: they have a starved spirit. They either refuse to feed themselves the essential nutrients, which the spirit needs in order to grow strong and healthy, or they are unable to do so. There is very little enjoyment of the glory of nature; they have little or no desire to read the Word of God, to fellowship with God's people and spending time in prayer is resisted.

The person with a starved spirit will almost always deny themselves the good things in life. Not for them the life of plenty. They can agree with St Paul about being 'in want' but they do not know what it means to 'abound'. They feel guilty if they are enjoying themselves. They deprive themselves and their families of the good things of life because in their spirit they feel unworthy.

One lady who had a starved spirit was given lots of lovely gifts at Christmas time, but because she felt unworthy inside, she put them to one side to give away during the following year. After much prayer we knew that she had been substantially healed when she visited the local town to buy herself clothes and jewellery that were normally totally out of bounds for her.

If you have a starved spirit there is normally a feeling that you must live a life of poverty. There will be a desire to live on the minimum; to be a part of the 'hair shirt brigade'. The 'bread and water diet' suits a person with this area of damage within their human spirit. Often there will be a sense of hopelessness and despair that seems to linger about the person.

Sometimes they become tied up in their body and soul because they are bound up in their spirit. They may become addicted to certain substances: alcohol, smoking, food or other kinds of addictive behaviour. Very often they will have a distorted view of themselves and many of them will suffer from bodily weaknesses. The writer of Psalm 109 knew something of this terrible condition:

> '*For I am poor and needy,*
> *And my heart is wounded within me.*
> *I am gone like a shadow when it lengthens;*
> *I am shaken off like a locust.*
> *My knees are weak through fasting,*
> *And my flesh is feeble from lack of fatness.*
> *I also have become a reproach to them;*
> *When they look at me, they shake their heads.'*
>
> (Psalm 109:22–25)

One wonders whether a starved spirit is responsible for the 'vague bodily pains' which plague people from time to time. The debilitating illness, chronic fatigue syndrome (sometimes called myalgic encephalomyelitis) could also spring from a starved spirit. However, many people develop ME after having the Epstein Barr virus or glandular fever; some people think that stress and depression are contributing factors. It could be that it is a combination of starved spirit, a virus and a life of stress.

Causes of a Starved Spirit

There are number of causes of a starved spirit. For example, if there has been an attempted abortion upon the child, a lie will have been sown into the child's spirit, 'You do not deserve to live.' That lie, until it is dealt with, could motivate the child throughout its life causing it to refuse to feed itself the good things of life which God intended.

One man who we prayed for had lost a twin at birth; he saw no purpose in life and suffered from deep depression for years. He felt guilty that he had lived and his brother had died. He is still in the process of accepting that he has a right to live. When there has been a measure of starvation or deprivation in the early years of life, this can also plant a sense of unworthiness within the human spirit. The person may then go on to reinforce this lack of self-worth by starving themselves of good things. For example, one woman, as a baby, was put to the breast regularly, but her mother never had enough milk. It was many days before this was realised by the nurses, but by then the damage had been done. She grew up with a starved spirit and needed much prayer in order for healing to flow.

However, any malnourishment can contribute to the condition. Being starved of affection; starved of security (like the child placed weekly in a dark cupboard as a means of punishment); or being starved of nurture. God means each child to know love, encouragement, a sense of worth and value, a knowledge of their significance and identity as well as knowing what it means to be cherished. If a person does not receive this loving nurture from their parents then very often there will be a deep sense of hunger in their spirit, which they feel must be normal and so they continue the pattern.

Early rejection, for example at the moment of conception or in the early months after birth, could lead to an inner vow of self-rejection: 'They don't want me therefore I don't want myself.' Such a person often chooses not to feed themselves spiritually, mentally or even physically and may be one reason for anorexic behaviour.

The above can become a 'control issue', usually as a result of being 'robbed' in some way when young, for example if a parent has died or essential physical nutrients were not fed down the umbilical cord.

Functions of the Starved Spirit

The functions of the human spirit which is starved will grow weak through lack of nurture. For example, the **creative** function begins to shrivel and the ability to feed **life** and **strength** into their body and soul and that of others becomes very inhibited. The ability to **communicate** spirit to spirit with others and with God is impeded.

Ministering to the Starved Spirit

- As with all ministry, it is very important to discern the root of the damage, because a lot of time can be wasted praying into the symptoms, and thus miss the real need.

- It will also be essential to feed and nurture the person's human spirit, little by little replacing what they have missed.
- This will include lots of fun things as well as spiritual activities. Give them permission to enjoy themselves.
- Take time to build up an atmosphere of trust because if they have suffered from any deprivation of affection or security they will find it easier to trust themselves.
- Break the power of the lie that 'they don't deserve to live'.
- As in every area of wounding within the human spirit, it is very important to speak the word of God to them.

A helpful psalm to read to a person with a starved spirit is Psalm 102. It is entitled in the New King James version 'A prayer of the afflicted, when he is overwhelmed and pours out his complaint before the LORD'. It truly sums up how they feel:

> *'Hear my prayer, O LORD,*
> *And let my cry come to You.*
> *Do not hide Your face from me in the day*
> *   of my trouble;*
> *Incline Your ear to me;*
> *In the day that I call, answer me speedily.*
>
> *For my days are consumed like smoke,*
> *And my bones are burned like a hearth.*
> *My heart is stricken and withered like grass,*
> *So that I forget to eat my bread.*
> *Because of the sound of my groaning*
> *My bones cling to my skin.*

I am like a pelican of the wilderness;
I am like an owl of the desert.
I lie awake,
And am like a sparrow alone on the housetop.

My enemies reproach me all day long,
Those who deride me swear an oath against me.
For I have eaten ashes like bread,
And mingled my drink with weeping . . .

He shall regard the prayer of the destitute,
And shall not despise their prayer.'

(Psalm 102:1–9, 17)

Chapter 5

Sinful Attitudes Arising from a Wounded Spirit

'The spirit of a man is the lamp of the LORD,
Searching all the inner depths of his heart.'
(Proverbs 20:27)

Let us consider the next question which we posed earlier: 'Does Scripture support the view that *sinful attitudes* can cause disease in the body?' I believe that all sin, whether of the flesh or of the soul, has its origin in man's inner being, in his human spirit, for truly it is out of the heart (the very centre of man's being) that the mouth speaks. The writer of Proverbs states about man:

'For as he thinks in his heart, so is he.'   (Proverbs 23:7)

Jesus would seem to confirm this:

'You have heard that it was said to those of old, "You shall not commit adultery." But I say to you that whoever looks at a woman to lust for her has already committed adultery with her in his heart.'

(Matthew 5:27–28)

In addition, in Matthew's Gospel, Jesus tells His disciples:

'For out of the heart proceed evil thoughts, murders, adulteries, fornications, thefts, false witness, blasphemies.'
(Matthew 15:19)

However, one might argue that the references are to the 'heart' and not to the 'human spirit'. Nevertheless, in Hebrew thinking 'heart and spirit' are very closely related. According to the *New Bible Dictionary* the heart is 'essentially the whole man, with all his attributes, physical, intellectual, and psychological, of which the Hebrew thought and spoke, and the heart was conceived of as the governing centre for all of these ... Character, personality, will, mind are modern terms which all reflect something of the meaning of 'heart' in its biblical usage'. When describing the sin of Adam the writer states that 'Sin was an event in the realm of the human spirit, but it has its repercussions in the whole of creation.' He also writes 'Sin never consists merely in a voluntary act of transgression. Every volition proceeds from something that is more deep-seated than the volition itself, and so it is with sinful volition ... Sin must always include, therefore, the perversity of heart, mind, disposition, and will.'[8]

Therefore, we would argue that certain sinful attitudes, whilst manifesting through the soul, actually proceed from the inner man, from the heart, from the spirit of the man. This is especially true when a person's spirit is wounded, for the damage may cause attitudes such as unforgiveness, resentment, anger, greed, envy, bitterness or remorse to become rooted in their very being. For example we may say about

---

[8]   *The New Bible Dictionary*, Inter-Varsity Press.

someone that 'she is a bitter woman', or that he is an 'angry or a greedy man'. This may, as we will see, go on to cause disease within the body.

Unforgiveness

For example, the paralysed man who was brought to Jesus by his friends:

> *'And behold, they brought to Him a paralytic lying on a bed. And Jesus, seeing their faith, said to the paralytic, "Son, be of good cheer; your sins are forgiven you."'*
>
> (Matthew 9:2)

Some sin had evidently caused his paralysis. Most doctors, whether Christian or secular, would see the importance of forgiveness as a vital element in healing, the necessity either for us to forgive others or to know forgiveness for ourselves.

The man at the pool of Bethesda was an invalid for thirty years and evidently sin had something to do with his illness:

> *'Afterward Jesus found him in the temple, and said to him, "See you have been made well. Sin no more, lest a worse thing come upon you."'*   (John 5:14)

Resentment

Resentment can certainly open the door to a number of diseases. The sister of Moses found this out to her cost when she, along with Aaron, began to usurp the leadership of Moses through resentment:

> *'And when the cloud departed from above the tabernacle,*
> *suddenly Miriam became leprous, as white as snow. Then*
> *Aaron turned toward Miriam, and there she was, a*
> *leper.'*   (Numbers 12:10)

Resentment is a sinful attitude, which can have far reaching effects in our physical frame. The preponderance of evidence seems to suggest that **some** incidents of mucous colitis have resentment as a root cause.

> 'A study at one hospital revealed, through personal interviews with patients suffering from mucous colitis, that resentment was the most prominent primary personality characteristic, occurring in ninety-six per cent of the victims.'   (George W. Gray)[9]

An ulcer can be the result of tension, anxiety, over work, an unreasonable boss, or an awkward marital partner, but internal resentment would certainly not help the condition, for resentment can produce a toxic reaction within one's body.

Unresolved Anger

It is important to note that not all anger is sinful. Some anger is totally justified; for example, we may get very angry at the injustices which are perpetrated against defenceless children. However, what we do with the anger determines how it will affect other people and even our own bodies. Deep, unresolved, excessive anger is a sinful attitude, which can cause disease within the body. According to St Paul we

[9]   George W. Gray, *Anxiety and Illness*, Harper's (May 1939), p. 610.

should *'Be angry, and do not sin'* (Ephesians 4:26). Paul also tells us not to let the sun go down on our wrath, probably knowing how nursing anger or a grudge overnight, never mind for days, weeks or even years, could damage our health irreparably.

In a recent article in the *Times* newspaper (12th March 2004) entitled 'Don't Blow Your Top' we are told that: 'A study published last week in the journal *Circulation* found that sulky men and those with bad tempers were 30% more likely to develop a dangerously irregular heartbeat (atrial fibrillation). Compared with calm men, angry men had a 20 per cent higher chance of dying from all causes.' The article continues, 'Four years ago a major heart journal reported that people prone to anger were nearly three times more likely to have a heart attack. Anger has since been linked to a worsening of irritable bowel disease, to ulcers, persistent headaches, sensitivity to pain, backache and arthritis.' The question is asked: 'Why should anger have such wide-ranging effects? Partly it's our old friend the stress response. "Hostile people have a chronically 'turned on' sympathetic nervous system," says Professor Catherine Stoney, a psychologist at Ohio State University, "This gives them higher blood pressure, higher heart rates and higher cholesterol."'

Doctors tell us that anger and rage are common factors in strokes. A famous physiologist John Hunter knew what anger could do to his heart. He said, 'The first scoundrel that gets me angry will kill me.' Some time later at a medical meeting a speaker made assertions that incensed Hunter. As he stood up and bitterly attacked the speaker, his anger caused such a contraction of the blood vessels in his heart that he fell down dead.

Anger can also cause high blood pressure. One woman had her blood pressure tested regularly. One day it soared from two hundred to two hundred and thirty. When the doctor asked her why, she smiled and said that she had just had an argument with another patient in the waiting room! She could have had a stroke.

Revenge

Linked with anger is the desire for revenge, which may be why the Lord emphasised that, *'Vengeance is mine. I will repay.'* He is more able to deal with it than we are. 'Man doesn't seem to learn that there is a high cost to pay in getting even, strokes and even heart attacks.'[10] In fact, if we want to stay healthy *'Love your enemy'* seems to be very good advice, never mind the admonition to love your neighbour!

Greed

Another sinful attitude which can cause disease is the sin of greed, as the story of Elisha's servant teaches us:

> *'Then he said to him, "Did not my heart go with you when the man turned back from his chariot to meet you? Is it time to receive money and to receive clothing, olive groves and vineyards, sheep and oxen, male and female servants? Therefore the leprosy of Naaman shall cling to you and your descendants forever." And he went out from his presence leprous, as white as snow.'*

(2 Kings 5:26–27)

[10] Dr S.I. McMillen, MD, *None of these Diseases*, Fleming H. Revell Co., Westwood, New Jersey.

Elisha's servant Gehazi lied and deceived Elisha and we see the disease that came upon him as a terrible consequence of his greed and deception. Please note that there is also a generational factor here, in that Gehazi's descendants were going to suffer physically for his sin as well. It is certainly possible for persistent characteristics or sinful attitudes of the spirit to be passed down the family line, i.e. anger, bitterness, resentment and depression. The reference to the blind man as recorded in John 9:2 is very interesting.

> *'And His disciples asked Him, saying, "Rabbi, who sinned, this man or his parents, that he was born blind?"'*

There is the suggestion that in Jesus' time the prevalent thought was that the sin of the parents could have caused the disease in their children. It is a well-documented fact that sometimes gonorrhoea passes down the family line and may cause blindness in future generations. This of course is not the only cause of blindness or other sight problems.

Remorse

In the story of Judas' betrayal, we see that it was remorse which ultimately caused his death.

> *'Then Judas, His betrayer, seeing that He had been condemned, was remorseful and brought back the thirty pieces of silver to the chief priests and elders, saying, "I have sinned by betraying innocent blood." And they said, "What is that to us? You see to it!" Then he threw down the pieces of silver in the temple and departed, and went and hanged himself.'* (Matthew 27:3–5)

142

A man who committed adultery on the evening of his wedding told no one about his sin and suffered from deep depression for forty years owing to his sense of remorse. It was only when he confessed and repented of his sin and received forgiveness that the depression lifted and healing followed.

Envy and Bitterness

Envy can cause a number of diseases within the body and we see a good example of this when the sorcerer Simon offered the Apostle Peter some money in order to be able to lay hands on people to receive the Holy Spirit. Peter discerned that his heart was not right before God and encouraged him to:

> *'Repent therefore of this your wickedness, and pray God if perhaps the thought of your heart may be forgiven you. For I see that you are poisoned by bitterness and bound by iniquity.'* (Acts 8:22–23)

His envy of what the apostles were able to do caused Simon to become very bitter in his spirit. Peter knew that unless he dealt with his envy it would have the potential of poisoning his body and his soul, for bitterness can eat away at a person like a cancer. According to Psychologist Henry C. Link, psychology has discovered a definite connection between sin and disease:

> 'The emphasis on sin has largely disappeared from the teachings of religion ... at the very time when psychology has discovered its importance and extended its meaning.'[11]

[11] Henry C. Link, *The Way to Security*, Garden City, New York, Doubleday & Co., Inc., 1951.

Chapter 6

Consequences of a Wounded Spirit

'In the day of my trouble I sought the Lord;
My hand was stretched out in the night
without ceasing;
My soul refused to be comforted.
I remembered God, and was troubled;
I complained, and my spirit was overwhelmed.
You hold my eyelids open;
I am so troubled that I cannot speak.'
(Psalm 77:2–4)

As we have seen when a person's spirit is wounded, it cannot feed into the soul and the body the comfort and the strength that they need in order to maintain health. Normally the soul is affected first (the mind, the emotions and the will) and the impairment is then filtered through into the body. Because the human spirit is unable to control the soul and the body, the soul endeavours to take charge. For example, the mind may try to gain control through compulsive thoughts, which then leads to obsessive behaviour. The will may try to cope by becoming addictive to certain substances or behaviour patterns.

It would appear that the emotions are particularly vulnerable (without the comforting strength and covering of the human spirit) and this has the potential of allowing disease to take root within the body. For example, when the emotions are stressed and anxious for an extended time, the body will undoubtedly feel the result and disease may ensue.

Anxiety and Stress

Anxiety and stress are very common emotions that continually plague humanity. According to the *Daily Express* (10th September 2003), 'the stresses of modern living are making us sick, doctors have warned. They believe increasing numbers of illnesses such as heart disease and diabetes are being brought on by our 24-hour world. Mobile phones, non-stop air travel and relentless trading across time zones are all adding to the problem.' Anne White in her book, *Healing Adventure*, writes that,

> 'Dr. Hans Selye, the Canadian Research Physiologist, has studied the effects of stress on the body's hormone production. The pituitary and adrenal glands release excess hormones in times of emotional or physical strain to meet the body's needs. However, if this is a chronic response, the overworking of these glands can lead to lowered resistance to disease. According to reports on Dr. Selye's experiments, the condition can be a significant factor in causing heart disease, hypertension, rheumatic fever and arthritis. Obviously, the deeper the person's consciousness of God, the more His peace can counteract the emotional and physical stresses and strains of life.'

There are many reasons for the very painful condition of fibromyalgia, a disease that the medical community refers to as pain in the muscles and tendons. They note that the condition occurs mainly in women and is sometimes accompanied by anxiety and stress. Whether the stress is a contributory factor to the disease or not, it is undoubtedly true that if the person is in a stressful situation it will aggravate the condition. There is no doubt that stress and its effects upon a person can be classified as a very serious illness, which many people have learnt to live with today.

Unfortunately it can also have serious consequences on the human body. Koo Stark, who wrote an article regarding the break-up of her marriage and the subsequent removal of her breast, says that her doctor told her that the stress of the break-up of her marriage could have contributed to her illness of breast cancer.

In his book *Living the Seven Habits*,[12] Stephen R. Covey tells the story of one young woman who developed lupus, an autoimmune disease that attacks the body's tissues. She and her brother were involved in an accident in which her brother suffered severe brain damage. She appeared to walk away unscathed. She was nine years old at the time. A year later she began to experience severe joint pains and was diagnosed with juvenile rheumatoid arthritis. During her junior year in high school the joint pains became much more severe and eventually after tests it was determined that she had systemic lupus-wolf. Doctors say that the accident, which she miraculously walked away from, could have been the **environmental stress** impact that resulted in the onset of this disease.

---

[12] Stephen R. Covey, *Living the Seven Habits*, Simon & Schuster UK Ltd, 2000.

Sometimes anxiety and stress can lead to depression:

'Anxiety in the heart of man causes depression,
But a good word makes it glad.'   (Proverbs 12:25)

The depression may be situated in the spirit, the soul or the body. If there is a physical cause for the depression, it could be because of a chemical imbalance and will need to be addressed accordingly with medical help. Conversely, it could be centred in the soul, caused by anger, guilt or other stressed emotions. However, if it has been caused by a wounding in the spirit, for example through a situation which has crushed or broken a person's spirit, then they would need prayer for healing for the human spirit, as well as for the depression. If the wounding is not dealt with then this could go on to have an adverse effect upon the soul and the body.

Stress and anxiety are not a natural part of God's intended order for humans: they affect our nervous system or over-work our adrenaline ducts; shingles, hives, and skin diseases may all be a result of stress and anxiety. In ulcerative colitis, the dendrites are inflamed, and stress and anxiety can contribute to this disease. We do not have an immune system against stress and anxiety, so we need a strategy to overcome them or disease may follow. One of the antidotes is to endeavour to be obedient to the commandment to love God with all of our hearts, for loving and trusting God as our Heavenly Father, as Jesus did, will help us to rest in His provision and His care for us. Jesus' strategy was to call His people to come unto Him and He would give them rest:

'Come to Me, all you who labour and are heavy laden,
and I will give you rest.'   (Matthew 11:28)

Fear

Fear is another very prevalent condition, which can cause disease in a person's body. According to a Methodist minister's wife, Elsie Salmon, who was greatly used in the healing ministry: 'Fear is the root cause of much sickness and disease; treat the cause and healing should follow.'[13] In the textbook *Pathophysiology: The Biologic Basis for Disease in Adults and Children*[14] it is stated that diseases such as angina and hypertension are considered fear, anxiety and stress diseases by the medical community.

Fear projects into the future and takes measures to avoid whatever we fear, whereas faith projects into the future and trusts God to bring it to pass. According to the writer of Hebrews,

> *'Faith is the substance of things hoped for, the evidence of things not seen.'* (Hebrews 11:1)

Whereas fear is the substance of things **not** hoped for, the evidence **not** yet seen – the antitheses of faith. Faith is a spiritual gift and it is the opposite to fear. It overcomes fear when God births it in our spirits.

The impact of fear on the body is very well known. In fact, we are told in Habakkuk that it can be so severe that,

> *'When I heard, my body trembled;*
> *My lips quivered at the voice.'* (Habakkuk 3:16)

[13] Elsie H. Salmon, *He Heals Today*, Arthur James, The Drift, Evesham.
[14] Kathryn L. McCance and Sue E. Huether, *Pathophysiology: The Biological Basis for Disease in Adults and Children*, 2nd edition, Mosby, 1994.

Fear can have so many physical repercussions: such as a trembling body, weak voice, a sudden dry throat, quivering lips and paralysis, to name but a few! It even seems possible for fear to produce a heart attack. According to some medical journals, one of the basic causes of many heart attacks is fear and anxiety. St Luke knew the truth of this many years ago when he wrote in his Gospel, *'men's hearts failing them from fear'* (Luke 21:26).

In the area of fear we are told that Job's fear caused all of his bones to shake,

> *'Fear came upon me, and trembling,*
> *Which made all my bones shake.'*   (Job 4:14)

There are a number of scriptures which seem to align 'bones with health', especially in the Psalms and in the book of Proverbs. For example,

> *'There is no soundness in my flesh*
> *Because of Your anger,*
> *Nor is there any health in my bones*
> *Because of my sin.'*   (Psalm 38:3)

> *'Do not be wise in your own eyes;*
> *Fear the* Lord *and depart from evil.*
> *It will be health to your flesh,*
> *And strength to your bones.'*   (Proverbs 3:7–8)

> *'A sound heart is life to the body,*
> *But envy is rottenness to the bones.'*   (Proverbs 14:30)

> *'The light of the eyes rejoices the heart,*
> *And a good report makes the bones healthy.'*
>   (Proverbs 15:30)

'Pleasant words are like a honeycomb,
Sweetness to the soul and health to the bones.'

(Proverbs 16:24)

The development of arthritis from fear and stress is also well known. Dr S.I. McMillen in his book *None of These Diseases*[15] says, 'we do not understand this mechanism but the fact of its occurrence is well known'. He tells the story of a farmer who one day consulted a doctor about a stomach complaint. The doctor noticed that the fingers on both of his hands were deformed with rheumatoid arthritis. He asked the man how long they had been like this. 'Ever since I was nine years old,' the man answered. Evidently there had been a panther scare in the neighbourhood when he was a young boy and he had to go through a dark and isolated wood. He had been very frightened thinking that the panther might jump out on him. After a couple of weeks his hands had begun to look deformed and they had stayed that way ever since. In the disease of rheumatoid arthritis the white corpuscles attack the joints and cartilage.

The foundation scripture for the healing of most fear disorders is to be found in 1 John 4:18:

'There is no fear in love; but perfect love casts out fear, because fear involves torment. But he who fears has not been made perfect in love.'

However, if a person's spirit is damaged then they will be unable to feed love into the soul and the body. It will need healing first.

[15]   Dr S.I. McMillen, MD, *None of These Diseases*, Fleming, H. Revell Company, Westwood, New Jersey.

Shame

Shame is another emotion which can cause problems in the physical area. According to Proverbs 12:4:

> '*An excellent wife is the crown of her husband,*
> *But she who causes shame is like rottenness in his*
>   *bones.*'

Very often when a person has been sexually abused or born out of wedlock, there is deep shame written in the spirit, and this too can cause disease in the soul or the body. We can see an illustration of this in the Scriptures when Amnon raped his half-sister Tamar:

> '*Now she* [Tamar] *had on a robe of many colours, for the king's virgin daughters wore such apparel. And his servant put her out and bolted the door behind her. Then Tamar put ashes on her head, and tore her robe of many colours that was on her, and laid her hand on her head and went away crying bitterly. And Absalom her brother said to her, "Has Amnon your brother been with you? But now hold your peace, my sister. He is your brother; do not take this thing to heart." So Tamar remained desolate in her brother Absalom's house.*'
>
> (2 Samuel 13:18–20)

I have prayed with a number of people who were illegitimate and who endured much shame throughout their lives. Many of them have also suffered from a number of physical infirmities. One woman, who continually walked around looking at the floor, shared with me that she had suffered from deep shame as long as she could remember. On sharing her story it appeared that she was born out of wedlock, and her grandmother had spoken scathing words over her whilst she was in the womb. She was born therefore in an atmosphere of shame and her body and soul could testify that the result was constant and changing illness. It was only when we prayed into the circumstances of her birth, asking that the Lord would forgive her parents' sin and lift the effects of her grandmother's words away from her spirit, that she began to look up and face life as God intended her to.

Another woman had difficulty looking anyone in the eye; she always evaded a straight look. Her husband had committed adultery and she bore the shame of other people's talk. Her back bore the result of the shame. From the moment she knew of his infidelity her back caused her frequent and excruciating pain. There was no healing for her back until she had forgiven her husband for his sin, forgiven herself for anything she had done to contribute to his unfaithfulness, and forgiven those who had spoken hurtfully against them. As God cleansed and healed her spirit, so the pain in her back began to ease.

Grief

Grief, of course, is a well-known emotion, which can cause physical disease, as well as terrible emotional turmoil. Maybe this is because unresolved grief can break a person's spirit:

> *'A merry heart makes a cheerful countenance,*
> *But by sorrow of the heart the spirit is broken.'*
>
> (Proverbs 15:13)

If a person's spirit is broken, then it will not be able to fulfil its job function of strengthening and supporting the soul and the body. It is imperative therefore for anyone trying to help someone through deep grief to remember that it is very important to bring healing to their spirit as well as to their body and soul.

The king took Nehemiah to task because he had a sorrowful face:

> *'Therefore the king said to me, "Why is your face sad, since you are not sick? This is nothing but sorrow of heart."'*   (Nehemiah 2:2)

However, he realised that the reason for the sadness of his face sprang from the inner sadness of his heart. The writer of Psalm 38:6–8 sums up what may be the physical effects of deep grief,

> *'I am troubled, I am bowed down greatly;*
> *I go mourning all the day long.*
> *For my loins are full of inflammation,*
> *And there is no soundness in my flesh.*
> *I am feeble and severely broken;*
> *I groan because of the turmoil of my heart.'*

We see that sorrow can cause sadness of face, a bent frame, inflammation of the loins, flesh becoming unsound, feebleness, inner turmoil, and dryness of bones. Dr S.I. McMillen, writes concerning a bereaved person,

> 'If chemical tests could have been made of her blood they would have disclosed the presence of a great

increase in hormones and abnormal toxins from the pituitary, thyroid, and adrenal glands. That something was present in toxic amounts is proven by the fact that next morning some of her fingers and her wrist joints were stiff, swollen, and painful. As well as the emotions of hate and resentment causing disease we see that the emotions of sorrow can also trigger disease in the body.'[16]

[16] Dr S.I. McMillen, MD, *None of These Diseases*, Fleming, H. Revell Company, Westwood, New Jersey.

Chapter 7

Spirit to Spirit Bonding

*'And it was so, when he had finished speaking to
Saul, that the soul of Jonathan was knit to the soul
of David, and Jonathan loved him as his own soul.'*
(1 Samuel 18:1)

We come now to the next very interesting question as
regards the role and the influence of the human spirit in
the area of health and disease. 'Could the health of my spirit
affect the health of someone to whom I am closely bonded,
or conversely could their spirit affect mine?' If the answer is
'yes' then the following question would also apply: 'Would
what is happening in the spirit of one person be able to affect
the other person physically or in their soul (i.e. mentally,
volitionally or emotionally)?'

Let me give you one or two examples to explain what I
mean. When there is a strong bonding between a parent
and a child this may allow what is happening in the spirit of
one of them to affect the spirit of the other. For example, a
certain couple had a child who died tragically at a very
young age. The husband loved his child deeply and had a
strong spirit bonding with her. Within a very short period
he also took ill and died. The wife always maintained that he

died of a broken heart caused by the premature death of his beloved daughter. When we consider the scripture: *'By sorrow of the heart the spirit is broken'* (Proverbs 15:13), one could believe that the father's spirit became so broken that like Job he could say:

> *'My spirit is broken,*
> *My days are extinguished,*
> *The grave is ready for me.'*   (Job 17:1)

In the same way the bonding between husband and wife, if it comes under undue strain, could cause problems spiritually, physically or emotionally in one or the other. One Christian couple, who had courted since school days and enjoyed a very happy marriage, were distraught when the woman suddenly contracted cancer and subsequently died. The husband, who was fit, healthy and of a cheerful personality, developed depression as a result and died within the year. Was this coincidence or could it be that what had happened to the wife had an adverse effect upon the spirit and consequently upon the mind and the body of the husband?

It is interesting to see the dynamics at work between King David and his wife Michal. She saw him dancing before the young maidservants and was incensed with his behaviour; the result was that she dishonoured him in her heart. Now according to the Scriptures, a wife should honour her husband, and King David's wife did just the opposite. God judged her for her wrong attitude, and the result had a remarkable effect upon her body in that she became barren. This scripture would seem to suggest that it is possible for sinful attitudes of the spirit, which are held against either husband or wife, could have a detrimental effect upon the soul and the body.

We have also noticed that when one of the partners either does not want a child, or withholds their spirit from the other during intercourse, that that has the potential of preventing pregnancy. It is important to emphasise however, that there are many other reasons for childlessness, some of which are purely physical.

One couple reported that for a number of months they fed one another 'negatively' in their spirits. The wife would wake up happy and positive ready to face a new day, only to suddenly become very depressed. When her husband returned home, after work, she was not surprised to find that he also had been struggling with depression. We have noted the negative effects of spirit to spirit bonding, but it must be stated that there can be a very positive input from one person to another as well.

In the book, *Emotionally Free*,[17] Kathy Mullen reports that she and her husband realised how very deeply connected they were in their spirits when Grant, her husband, felt the presence of God really strongly at home, while at the very same time, she found herself overcome by the presence of God in church. Friends of long standing, siblings or twins also know the truth that it is possible to be so close to one another in their spirits that they can influence each other for good or ill. Maybe that is why so many couples, friends, or family have the ability to finish sentences for one another!

[17] Grant Mullen, MD, *Emotionally Free*, Sovereign World.

Chapter 8

Sustaining the Soul and the Body

'The spirit of a man will sustain him in sickness.'
(Proverbs 18:14)

The question concerning the part which the human spirit plays in sustaining the health of the soul and the body is this: 'Is it the job of the ***human spirit*** to help the soul and the body when they become ill?' According to the writer of the book of Proverbs, it certainly would appear to be so:

'The spirit of a man will sustain him in sickness.'
(Proverbs 18:14)

However, if the spirit is wounded or weak, it will be unable to fulfil this job function. Much spiritual suffering may be added to the suffering of the soul and the body. Conversely, if the spirit is strong and healthy then it can bring much help to the person, even in the face of death.

A very good friend of ours developed cancer late in life. Eventually she was moved to a hospice and we went to visit her. She was in surprisingly good spirits considering she was facing death. She said, 'Many people are praying for my healing, but I have to tell you Ruth, that if God takes me tonight I will be delighted to go to Him. My body is getting weaker every day, but my spirit, oh my spirit is so much stronger than it has ever been, and it is encouraging my body to be prepared for God's call.'

We heard recently of a very bright, elderly, Christian man who has become confused in his mind. However, he is perfectly lucid if you start to quote a scripture, sing a hymn, or pray with him. Truly, his spirit is strengthening his soul and his body. Likewise, a friend of ours, who for a number of months was in a coma, would mouth the Scriptures with anyone who was reading the Bible to him.

A Christian doctor spent a number of hours reading the twenty-third Psalm to a woman who was in a coma because of a serious road accident. She was not a professing Christian but God had given him a burden of prayer for her. He based his actions on the premise that the human spirit never sleeps and therefore she would 'hear in her spirit' the life giving Word of God. His testimony is that whilst he knows that the doctors in the hospital did a tremendous job of aiding the woman's healing, he also believes that God so strengthened the woman's spirit that eventually when she came out of the coma her progress was so much quicker.

Ruth Calver, wife of Clive Calver, a well known Christian leader, wrote an article for a Christian journal concerning how one day she was praying with her mother-in-law, who had Alzheimer's disease. She suggested that her mother-in-law might also like to pray. 'At this point she had no power of speech, other than the occasional grunt. Amazingly she prayed, "Dear Lord Jesus, I don't know who I am, I don't know what I am, I don't know where I am, but please love me." Never again was she able to form a sentence.' Truly, the human spirit was strengthening her soul and her body.

Elsie was in her early fifties when her doctor told her that she had a terminal illness. On asking how long she had to live, she was told that at the most it would be nine months to a year. Elsie had a problem; her only daughter was getting married in eighteen months time and Elsie was determined to see her married and settled. 'No way' was the prognosis from the doctor, but Elsie fulfilled her desire and died two months after her daughter was wed. What kept her going? How did she defeat the timeline, which should have been her due? Surely, it was because her spirit was strong although her body was getting weaker, and it strengthened her body and soul in order for her longing to be rewarded. Truly in this and the above instances the truth of Scripture was proved:

> *'The spirit of a man will sustain him in sickness.'*
>
> (Proverbs 18:14)

It would seem therefore to be very important to know **how** to maintain our human spirit in a state of health in the good times, in order for it to do its job in the bad times. For example, if our spirit is damaged in any way i.e. crushed, broken, defiled, timid or imprisoned, then we will need to know how to seek prayer ministry in order for the Holy Spirit to bring our human spirits to a place of healing.[18] It is also very important to know some of the keys which will enable a person to continue to walk in health. We will look at several of them in chapter 10.

---

[18] For more understanding in this area we would suggest the following two books: *Comfort for the Wounded Spirit* by Frank and Ida Hammond and *Healing the Human Spirit* by Ruth Hawkey, both of which are published by New Wine Press.

Chapter 9

Praying for the Wounded in Spirit

'But I have prayed for you.'
(Luke 22:32)

Spirit to Spirit

As we have noted in chapter 7 on 'Spirit to Spirit Bonding', it is possible to be so closely aligned with another person that what happens in one person's spirit will have an impact upon the other. This, as we have seen, can be either for good or ill.

When we are praying for people who are wounded in their human spirit, there are two very significant observations, which I want to make:

1. It is very important to be spiritually open to the person who is in need of prayer.
2. We need to know how to protect our own human spirit whilst this is happening.

The reason why this is so important is that for healing to be effective there needs to be a 'spirit to spirit' encounter. Tom

Marshall, who has written a number of excellent books about the healing ministry, first introduced me to the concept of 'living out of the spirit', of drawing near to people and touching them through our human spirit.

Jesus knew how to approach people, 'spirit to spirit': He 'knew', He 'saw', and He 'discerned.' He intuitively knew what people were thinking and feeling through His human spirit and responded accordingly. Because this is such a crucial subject, I want to give you a number of examples from the Scriptures. Jesus understood 'spiritually' the shame of the woman who was caught in the act of adultery. He understood intuitively in His spirit the pride of her accusers and the fact of universal sin:

> *'So when they continued asking Him, He raised Himself up and said to them, "He who is without sin among you, let him throw a stone at her first."'* (John 8:7)

When Jesus met the leper, He 'discerned' the man's unspoken need, which was to feel a human touch, for they were the 'untouchables'.

> *'Then a leper came to Him, imploring Him, kneeling down to Him and saying to Him, "If You are willing, You can make me clean." And Jesus, moved with compassion, put out His hand and touched him, and said to him, "I am willing; be cleansed."'* (Mark 1:40–41)

Jesus 'saw' the hardness of heart of those who were against Him healing on the Sabbath day and purposely stood against it:

> *'So when He had looked around at them with anger, being grieved by the hardness of their hearts, He said to the man, "Stretch out your hand." And he stretched it out, and his hand was restored as whole as the other."'*
>
> (Mark 3:5)

There is the occasion when Jesus 'knew in His spirit' that someone had touched Him spiritually as well as physically:

> *'And Jesus, immediately knowing in Himself that power had gone out of Him, turned around in the crowd and said, "Who touched My clothes?"'* (Mark 5:30)

To the woman with the issue of blood He 'saw' her desperate longing to be affirmed as part of humanity:

> *'And He said to her, "Daughter, your faith has made you well. Go in peace, and be healed of your affliction."'*
>
> (Mark 5:34)

Thus, we see from the Scriptures that Jesus was able to read people's spirits and was able to react in an appropriate manner. He was spiritually aware, and this responsiveness triggered a reaction in His soul, either a volitional, mental or emotional response (i.e. anger, compassion, love) which then resulted in an appropriate action.

Learning to Live 'Spirit to Spirit'

Like Jesus, we also can reach out and spiritually touch another wounded and hurting person. We can learn how to communicate with our spirit as well as with our soul and our

163

body: a hug, a touch and a smile are all expressions of love, which we can use to express the love of the Father to the wounded in spirit.

However, we can also learn how to reach out and *specifically* touch another person's spirit. Many of us do this automatically in our friendships, marriages, and fellowships. We intuitively know when we are in deep spiritual communion with another person, be that a spouse, a good friend or one of our children. We need to recognise the possibility of this happening in a ministry situation as well. Most of us know instinctively whether we have touched spirit to spirit or not. We must emphasise again that this is open to abuse and any ministry team person must learn how to protect their spirits, and where to seek help if they do pick up any spiritual pollution.

The Place of Compassion

Compassion is the doorway through which our human spirit touches another person's spirit. It is vital to be able to empathise with the one in need of prayer ministry if we are going to be effective in bringing them to a place of healing. Jesus continually ministered into people's spirits in this way and it is noted time and again that, 'He had compassion on them'. The following are some examples:

▶ *The man who was born blind*

> *'They said to Him, "Lord, that our eyes may be opened."
> So Jesus had compassion and touched their eyes. And
> immediately their eyes received sight, and they followed
> Him.'* (Matthew 20:33–34)

▶ *Those with leprosy*

> *'And Jesus, moved with compassion, put out His hand and touched him, and said to him, "I am willing; be cleansed."'* (Mark 1:41)

▶ *The lost and the leaderless*

> *'And Jesus, when He came out, saw a great multitude and was moved with compassion for them, because they were like sheep not having a shepherd.'* (Mark 6:34)

▶ *The bereaved widow*

> *'And when He came near the gate of the city, behold, a dead man was being carried out, the only son of his mother; and she was a widow. And a large crowd from the city was with her. When the Lord saw her, He had compassion on her and said to her, "Do not weep."'*
> (Luke 7:12–14)

Some General Guidelines

When ministering into the human spirit the following are some of the points which should be noted:

- Recognise that your human spirit has certain job functions and be willing to use them on behalf of those for whom you are praying.
- Recognise the need to be continually filled with the Holy Spirit, so that the functions of your human spirit will be directed and empowered by Him.

- Learn to trust your **intuition**, to listen to that still small voice within and in prayer ministry be led by it, for this is how and where we receive the gifts of the Holy Spirit i.e. words of knowledge and discernment. We must, of course, test what we hear by the Word of God and the affirmation of other mature Christians.

At the close of a teaching seminar on 'Healing the Human Spirit,' a woman, who was visiting Britain from abroad, approached us on behalf of her son. She was very concerned for her boy, who was dyslexic and whose sensory and motor co-ordination was lower than that of children of the same age. She asked me how she should pray into her situation. I had no definite guidance but quickly sent up a 'help' prayer to the Lord. Trusting Him for wisdom, I encouraged her to pray into his human spirit and to refer to the psychologist and occupational therapists' diagnosis of the boy's case – praying a supernatural anointing into what the medical people had discerned.

When I met her several months later, she told me that she and a friend had agreed in prayer to pray as I had suggested. Ten days later she telephoned her husband to hear that he had received a report from the principal of her son's school, to say that his grades had improved dramatically. He was seventeen when she started to pray for him. He is now twenty and is studying law and coping very well. She gives all of the glory to the Lord. We need to learn to trust our intuition, testing it alongside the Scriptures.

- Learn how to feed **life, comfort, strength** and **encouragement** into those for whom you are praying. Words are very powerful in this context.

- Learn how to use your **creative** faculty. The Almighty God, who is the 'uncreated Creator', created the world through His Word:

  > *'By faith we understand that the worlds were framed by the word of God, so that the things which are seen were not made of things which are visible.'*
  >
  > (Hebrews 11:3)

Moreover, according to Genesis chapter 1, we repeatedly have the words, *'And God Said . . . and it was so'*. Since we are made in the image of God, we are 'created creators' and we have the ability to speak into being God's purposes for the person in need. Through faith we are able to speak words of healing into them, to speak truth into their situation or to declare God's forgiveness on confession of their sin.

- Learn how to move under the **anointing of the Holy Spirit**. Prayer ministry must be led by the Holy Spirit from beginning to end. Just as Jesus moved under the anointing of the Holy Spirit so must we.

  > *The Spirit of the* Lord *is upon Me,*
  > *Because He has anointed Me to preach the*
  >   *gospel to the poor;*
  > *He has sent Me to heal the brokenhearted,*
  > *To preach deliverence to the captives*
  > *And recovery of sight to the blind,*
  > *To set at liberty those who are oppressed.'*
  >
  > (Luke 4:18)

An elderly man in his late seventies, from a local Baptist church, visited a conference where we were teaching 'Healing the Human Spirit'. At the close of the conference he heard someone sobbing and to his intense surprise discovered it was himself! He had no ministry; did not share his story with anyone at the time; cried for over half an hour and felt that he could only share what had happened many weeks later. It was, he said, 'the wonderful presence of the Holy Spirit that impacted my spirit, the anointing was so powerful and yet so gentle.'

- Learn how to be a **facilitator** through which the Holy Spirit can touch the human spirit of the person to whom you are ministering. The Holy Spirit will breathe into your spirit and use your spirit to reach out and touch the other person in their spirit. As we have seen this means that your spirit must be open to the Holy Spirit and be prepared to receive from Him whatever He seeks to do for the other person. It must also be open to the other person. Let me re-emphasise, however, the necessity of knowing how to guard your spirit especially if it is very sensitive.
- Learn how to use the many **tools** which God has given to His Body, the Church. Undoubtedly the most important of these is the Word of God:

> '... *the sword of the Spirit, which is the word of God.*'
> (Ephesians 6:17)

Through the Word of God people's lives can be dramatically changed. Jesus says that His words are 'life-giving':

> '*The words that I speak to you are spirit, and they are life.*'
> (John 6:63)

Another tool is the sword of our own human spirit; Scripture affirms that our tongue is also a sword:

> *'And their tongue a sharp sword.'* (Psalm 57:4)

Our words are meant to encourage, affirm, build up, challenge and speak truth, as does the Word of God, the sword of the Holy Spirit. The writer of the book of Proverbs knew the power of this sword:

> *'Death and life are in the power of the tongue.'*
> (Proverbs 18:21)

There are many references in the Scriptures to the power of the tongue, one of which is that our tongue is a tree of life:

> *'A wholesome tongue is a tree of life.'* (Proverbs 15:4)

The 'tree of life' reference is very interesting when you consider the other references to this tree in the Scriptures:

> *'The tree of life was also in the midst of the Garden.'*
> (Genesis 2:9)

> *'In the middle of its street, and on either side of the river, was the tree of life ... And the leaves of the tree were for the healing of the nations.'* (Revelation 22:2)

In the book of Ezekiel, as regards the tree of life, we are told that:

> *'... Their fruit will be for food, and their leaves for medicine.'* (Ezekiel 47:12)

Our words therefore are very powerful, and as a 'sword' we need to learn how to direct our words into the other person's spirit: to speak life into the one needing prayer. This is especially life-enhancing when we mingle our words with the Word of God.

The gifts of the Holy Spirit are of course vital in prayer ministry, especially the ability to speak in the language of the Holy Spirit. Jackie Pullinger, who worked in Hang Fook Camp in Hong Kong, used this tool very effectively on behalf of the former drug addicts amongst whom she worked. As she prayed into their spirits, bypassing their minds, which were probably befuddled with drugs, her testimony was that they matured very quickly in their faith.

Specifically we need to ask the Holy Spirit to find the area of the person's spirit which is hurt and wounded, and if there is any specific memory connected with that wounding, to bring it to the surface. You will need to be prepared to wait expectantly and patiently for this to happen. Expect the Holy Spirit to give words of knowledge, either to you or to the other person. Keep looking for the roots of the damage and pray specifically into them.

The Holy Spirit led us to pray for one man who had a crushed spirit. He was a very angry man, and had been all of his life. During prayer the Lord directed us to enquire about his birth. Evidently he had been one of twins and his identical twin had been stillborn. The Lord shared with us that this was the root of his anger and that the deep loss had crushed his spirit at the moment of birth. We left him in the safe hands of his Church Prayer Ministry team to pray and care for him.

When ministering to particular areas of damage it is very important to note the following:

- Always look for the root of the damage
- Be aware of the likelihood of the demonic being present
- Depend always upon the Holy Spirit to lead the ministry, for there is no technique
- Be open to using the gifts of the Holy Spirit
- You will need to break any ungodly bondings which have been formed
- Use the Word of God, for it is a powerful tool.

The following are some scriptures which we have found useful when praying into the various conditions of the human spirit:

▶ *The timid spirit*

> '... *perfect love casts out fear.*' (1 John 4:18)

> '*I sought the* Lord, *and He heard me,*
> *And delivered me from all my fears.*' (Psalm 34:4)

▶ *The starved spirit*

> '*To console those who mourn in Zion,*
> *To give them beauty for ashes,*
> *The oil of joy for mourning,*
> *The garment of praise for the spirit of heaviness.*'
> (Isaiah 61:3)

> '*When my spirit was overwhelmed within me,*
> *Then You knew my path.*' (Psalm 142:3)

> *To loose those appointed to death.* (Psalm 102:20b)

▶ *The imprisoned spirit*

> *'To proclaim liberty to the captives.'* (Isaiah 61:1)

> *'You shall know the truth and the truth shall set you free.'* (John 8:32)

> *'God sets the solitary in families.'* (Psalm 68:6)

> *'From heaven the* L ORD *viewed the earth,*
> *To hear the groaning of the prisoner,*
> *To loose those appointed to death.'* (Psalm 102:19–20)

▶ *The crushed spirit*

> *'A bruised reed He will not break.'* (Isaiah 42:3)

▶ *The orphaned spirit*

> *'You are the helper of the fatherless.'* (Psalm 10:14)

> *'A father of the fatherless.'* (Psalm 68:5)

> *'But as many as received Him, to them He gave the right to become children of God.'* (John 1:12)

> *'When my father and my mother forsake me,*
> *Then the* L ORD *will take care of me.'* (Psalm 27:10)

▶ *The defiled spirit*

> *'. . . the blood of Jesus Christ His Son cleanses us from all sin.'* (1 John 1:7)

'I will sprinkle clean water on you, and you shall be clean; I will cleanse you from all your filthiness and from all of your idols.' (Ezekiel 36:25)

'how much more shall the blood of Christ ... purge your conscience.' (Hebrews 9:14)

▶ *The broken spirit*

'[Jesus came] ... *'to heal the brokenhearted.'*
(Isaiah 61:1; see also Luke 4:18)

*'The LORD is near to those who have a broken heart,
And saves such as have a contrite spirit.'* (Psalm 34:18)

It is of course very important to remember to pray for physical healing for the person if you discern that damage to the human spirit has caused or contributed to their ill health. A number of months ago we were asked to pray for a woman who had suffered bodily injury in a car accident. Her back and her knees were affected. She had had a lot of prayer into the physical injuries but was still suffering from much pain. After sharing her story with us, we discerned that the shock and the trauma of the accident had affected her human spirit and sealed in the wounding to her body. We asked the Lord to take her back to the time of the accident (He is the same yesterday, today and forever), and bring healing into her human spirit. We asked Him to lift away shock, trauma, fear and stress from her spirit, soul and body. We commanded any demonic spirits to depart in the name of Jesus. We then prayed for the physical healing of her back and her knees. Next morning she reported that she had no more pain and was convinced that the Lord had indeed healed her.

Chapter 10

Some Keys to Healthy Living

'Pleasant words are like a honeycomb,
Sweetness to the soul and health to the bones.'
(Proverbs 16:24)

We come now to our final question: 'Are there any *keys to healthy living*?' We could of course list many practical suggestions: eating well, taking plenty of exercise, making sure we have good sleep patterns, good housing etc., but we want to allude to the ones which we feel are the most significant within the context of this book: **spiritual keys**. One of the prayers which St Paul prays for the Christians in Thessalonica is the following,

> '... *may your whole spirit, soul, and body be preserved blameless at the coming of our Lord Jesus Christ.'*
>
> (1 Thessalonians 5:23)

Or as The Living Bible translates this verse:

> '... *may your spirit and soul and body be kept strong and blameless.'*

We would propose that for a person to live in a healthy manner, it is vital that attention be given, not only to the condition of the soul and the body, but also to the state of the human spirit. There are many ways to strengthen and improve the health of the spirit, for example by meditating on the Word of God, through Christian fellowship, by prayer and partaking in the sacraments. We understand that it is only possible to put the following keys into practice when our human spirit is continually strengthened and submitted to the Holy Spirit.

The Scriptures teach us that one of the primary **keys to healthy living** is for us to make peace with God, with our neighbours and with ourselves. In other words to walk in obedience to His command to:

> '... *"love the* LORD *your God with all your heart, with all your soul, and with all your mind." This is the first and great commandment. And the second is like it: "You shall love your neighbour as yourself." On these two commandments hang all the Law and the Prophets.'*
> (Matthew 22:37–40)

If we **love God** with all of our being then when we do sin, as we will as frail human beings, we will want to keep a short account with God. Thus guilt and remorse will be dealt with at the cross and will no longer have the power to cause disease in the soul and the body.

Because of our love for Him we will swiftly confess any known, specific sin, first to God and then to any other person whom it may have affected. The Apostle James thus encourages us that:

> '... *if he has committed sins, he will be forgiven.'*
> (James 5:15)

He encourages us to *'confess your trespasses to one another'* (James 5:16), for this opens the door to the Lord being able to 'mend' us as we saw in Exodus 15:26, *'I am the LORD who heals you.'*

As well as loving God we are also commanded to **love other people**. This is another significant *key to healthy living*. God knows that if we love our neighbours then we will choose to walk in forgiveness towards them and the sinful attitudes of bitterness, resentment, revenge, greed, envy and jealousy will not be able to take root and cause problems in our souls and our bodies. This offer of **forgiveness** to other people for any sins which they have committed against us (which must be from the heart, although sometimes will begin as a choice from the will), is fundamental to our health. As God forgives us, so we are commanded to forgive other people. Jesus included this command in the Lord's Prayer:

> *'And forgive us our sins,*
> *For we also forgive everyone who is indebted to us.'*
>
> (Luke 11:4)

Thus when we forgive others we are obeying His command-ment and healing can follow.

> *'Who forgives all your iniquities,*
> *Who heals all your diseases.'* (Psalm 103:3)

In the early nineties we were privileged to be present at a conference in Hungary where there were delegates from Eastern Europe. At first there was a definite feeling of suspicion amongst the people, even though they were

Christians. Their past history of anger, hate and even murder, which many had experienced in their families, was very much in evidence. This suspicion only lifted after a period of repentance, forgiveness and very sensitive worship. It was as though the joining of their spirits, especially through the worship, fed them and freed them from the mistrust, which had built up over the years. As the writer to the Corinthians says, *'knowledge puffs up, but love edifies'* (1 Corinthians 8:1), and certainly in this instance love eventually broke through the barriers and united their hearts.

Another important **key to healthy living** is also summed up in this commandment, for we are told that we must also **love ourselves**. It is this decree which most of us find very difficult to obey. It appears to be much easier to love God and other people than it is to love ourselves. There are many reasons for this: low self-esteem, self-rejection, and our past parenting to name but a few. However, the acceptance of oneself cannot be overemphasised in the area of walking in health, and it is worth spending time in order to arrive at the place of acceptance. It may be, of course, that we will need other people to work with us in this area. We were told in a newspaper report in the *Daily Mail* (19th November 2001) by Dr Andrew Weil that: 'the most common correlation I observe between mind and healing in people suffering from chronic illness is the total acceptance of the circumstances of one's life, including illness. This "letting go" allows a profound internal relaxation, so that the patient need no longer feel compelled to maintain a defensive stance towards life ... Acceptance, submission, surrender – whatever one chooses to call this mental shift – may be the master key that unlocks healing.'

The psychiatrist Smiley Blanton in his book *Love or Perish* says that: 'Love is the one and only antidote that can save man from the many diseases produced by the emotions of our evil nature. Without love man is likely to perish from a number of diseases of mind or body.'[19] To love God, yourself and your neighbour is as relevant today as it was in the days of Moses!

Having **faith** in the goodness, mercy and sovereignty of God is another major *key to healthy living*. When we realise how much God loves us: *'We love Him because He first loved us'* (1 John 4:19), then we come to a settled place of quiet confidence and trust in Him for our future well being. Thus having the faith that God has both the desire to heal us and the power to do so is a priority in restoring a healthy spirit, soul and body. Remember that faith comes by hearing and hearing comes by the Word of God. The Apostle James reminds us that:

> *'... the prayer of faith will save the sick, and the Lord will raise him up.'* (James 5:15)

According to *Newsweek* magazine (24th September 1990), 'Healthy thinking may eventually become an integral aspect of treatment for everything from allergies to liver transplants and prevention of disease.' Christians would say that this is another definition of faith!

It was reported in the *Times* newspaper (3rd September 2002) that: 'the new science of psycho-neuroimmunology, founded after the discovery in the 1970s of endorphin receptors in the brain, has identified "numerous routes by which the immune and central nervous systems communicate", says

[19] Smiley Blanton, *Love or Perish*, New York, Simon and Schuster, Inc., 1956.

Esther Sternberg, director of the US National Institute of Mental Health's integrative neural immune programme, suggesting "mechanisms by which factors such as beliefs and expectations may influence neuro-endocrine and neural responses which could, in turn, affect immune responses and disease expression or severity'.

It also said that: 'an analysis of trials of antidepressants published in 1998 and entitled 'Listening to Prozac but Hearing Placebo', found the placebo response was twice as powerful as the active ingredient. In the year 2000, ulcer patients who were given four different placebo tablets a day, had a higher rate of healing (endoscopically verified) than those taking one or two placebos. It was also found that taking tablets regularly makes them more effective. This is true of placebos as well as active drugs, according to studies of antibiotics and anti-psychotics. Truly a case of having faith in the tablets!

It is interesting to note the important place which **laughter** has in promoting health. The ability to laugh with others and at oneself is a tremendous *key to healthy living*. According to the writer to Proverbs:

'A merry heart does good, like medicine.'
(Proverbs 17:22)

It has been soundly documented that laughter causes the body to manufacture T cells and killer cells, which fight off disease as well as strengthening the immune system.

Being **led by the Holy Spirit** is a major *key to healthy living*. When we are led by the Holy Spirit we come into a rightful submission to the Heavenly Father and this restores our human spirit into the proper godly authority structure:

the Holy Spirit guiding and strengthening the human spirit which then guides and strengthens the soul and the body. It all begins and ends with obedience and submission to the commandments of God. This is the prayer of St Paul for the Christians in Ephesus:

> *'For this reason I bow my knees to the Father of our Lord Jesus Christ, from whom the whole family in heaven and earth is named, that He would grant you, according to the riches of His glory, to be strengthened with might through His Spirit in the inner man.'*   (Ephesians 3:14–16)

It is also the prayer of St Paul for the Christians in Thessalonica that:

> *'. . . the God of peace Himself sanctify you completely; and may your whole spirit, soul, and body be preserved blameless at the coming of our Lord Jesus Christ.'*
>
> (1 Thessalonians 5:23)

There is a very real sense in which our human spirit needs to be sanctified and strengthened, because it is only when that happens that our souls and our bodies will come into line with the Holy Spirit, and will begin to submit to the Word of God.

As we have already stated there are many reasons for disease:

> 'Suffering is a human experience, with diverse causes, and is one of the results of human sin.'[20]

[20]   J.D. Douglass, MA, BD, STM, PhD, *The New Bible Dictionary*, Inter-Varsity Press.

Our premise is that the sins and wounds of the human spirit could be one of those causes. It would seem to be very important, therefore, that we continue to explore the role of the human spirit to see whether this is one of God's keys to healing, for we believe that He is still 'Jehovah Rapha' – the God who heals.

Appendix

'Where Does Life Live?'

As we have stressed in the preface to this book, we are **exploring** the concept of how our health may, in some instances, be affected by the state of our human spirit. We would especially ask you to read this appendix in the light of it being an investigation of the subject, rather than a finished article. We are still in the process of learning and merely want to share our thinking with you.

According to the Scriptures the primary function of the human spirit is to communicate life to the soul and the body. Our premise is that if that life is defective then disease may be the result and that when that life departs then death happens. We read in the letter of James that, *'the body without the spirit is dead'* (James 2:26).

On observation of a dead body, we realise that the spirit of the person has departed. All that is left is the empty shell. Ralph O. Muncaster, in his book *Dismantling Evolution*, asks some very relevant questions concerning what 'life' actually is. In the second chapter he tells the story of a six-year-old girl who is injured by a speeding vehicle and is very close to death. He writes, 'Then for a few heart-wrenching minutes, her life seemed to have slipped away. Was Ashley really dead? Or, as the doctors were scrambling to "restart" her heart, was her brain still working, waiting for her heart to start pumping and delivering oxygen again?' He goes on to ask some very important questions. 'So what is death, really? And what is life, really?' He follows this up with what to us is an even more relevant question: 'where does life "live"?'[21]

The Scriptures would seem to suggest that there are at least two possible answers to that question, the first one being that life is in the blood,

> '... *the life of the flesh is in the blood ...* '
> (Leviticus 17:11)

From this we could deduct that the life, which is imparted to the soul and the body from the human spirit, is fed into the body via the blood. The quality of that life may determine the health and the wellbeing of the body. Note that by saying 'life is in the blood' we are not suggesting (and I don't believe that Scripture suggests it either) that 'life' and 'blood' are synonymous. Please forgive this simple illustration, but if you put a tea bag in water, we understand that they are both distinctive entities. It is possible to remove the tea bag (the life of the spirit) and leave the water (the blood) or vice-versa.

According to H. Wheeler Robinson, there are many references in the Scriptures concerning the 'mystery of life indwelling in the blood'. For example,

> '*But you shall not eat flesh with its life, that is, its blood.*'
> (Genesis 9:4)

---

[21] Ralph O. Muncaster, *Dismantling Evolution*, Harvest House Publishers, Eugene, Oregon, 2003.

He also states that, according to Hebrew psychology, 'man's consciousness, with its ethical qualities, was thought to be so diffused through the whole body that the flesh and bones, as well as the mouth, eye, ear, hand, had a quasi-consciousness of their own'.[22] Whether this was a true understanding or not, certainly the way for it to be achieved would be via the blood coursing through the body, for the chief function of the blood is to carry oxygen to the tissues where the oxygen is used in energy-producing chemical processes. Then the waste products of these processes (the carbon dioxide) is picked up by the blood and returned to the lungs to be breathed out. God has put an important emphasis upon the blood. It percolates taking life, oxygen and nutrients to each part of your body. It swills out disease.

There is also a great emphasis upon the importance of the blood in the Scriptures. In fact, the blood was so significant to the Jewish people that they were forbidden to eat anything with blood in it,

> *'And whatever man of the house of Israel, or of the strangers who dwell among you, who eats any blood, I will set My face against that person who eats blood, and will cut him off from among his people.'*   (Leviticus 17:10)

Why is it so important not to eat anything with blood in it? It would seem to be because the life of the animal is in the blood and that lifeblood is God's alone: He will not allow anyone to steal that life from Him.

A peculiar sacredness was attached to blood because of the idea that prevailed of its unity with the soul. According

---

[22] 'Hebrew Psychology', H. Wheeler Robinson in *The People and the Book*, A.S. Peake (ed.), Oxford University Press.

to Delitzsch (*The New Unger's Bible Dictionary*): 'This identification of the blood with the soul, which prevailed in antiquity, appears at first to have no further foundation than that a sudden diminution of the quantity of blood in the body causes death. However, this phenomenon itself has the deeper reason that all activity of the body depends on the quantity of the blood. The blood is actually the basis of the physical life; and, so far, the soul, as the principle of bodily life, is pre-eminently in the blood.'

From the Scriptures, therefore, it would appear that the term 'blood' signifies life. It is important to note however, that other people may hold a different point of view. According to *The New Bible Dictionary*, 'There are those who hold that in the sacrificial system of the Old Testament "blood" represents life liberated from the limitations of the body and set free for other purposes'. However, the writer leans to the view that 'death is the association most likely to be conjured up by the use of the term'.[23]

The Importance of the Bones

The second answer to the question: 'Where does life "live"?' is suggested in chapter 37 of the book of Ezekiel which deals with the valley of dry bones. The suggestion is that life resides in the bones,

> *'The hand of the LORD came upon me and brought me out in the Spirit of the LORD, and set me down in the midst of the valley; and it was full of bones.'*

> (Ezekiel 37:1)

---

[23] *The New Bible Dictionary*, Inter-Varsity Press, 1962.

According to the *Wycliffe Bible Commentary*, Ezekiel is told to prophesy to the **bones** the promise of life. ' *"I will cause breath to enter into you."* The Hebrew word *ruach* is translated "breath" in verses 5, 6 ,8, 9, 10, "winds" in verse 9, and "spirit" in verses 1, 14. The context usually determines the translation. Breath is a sign of life, identical with wind or air, and becomes, in this prophecy, the living principle itself, spirit.'[24]

Adam Clarke's Commentary would seem to confirm this interpretation. He gives a breakdown of Ezekiel 37:6 (AV):

> '*And I will lay sinews upon you, and will bring up flesh upon you, and cover you with skin, and put breath in you, and ye shall live; and ye shall know that I am the LORD.*'

He writes, '[I will lay sinews upon you] Observe the progress:

1. Here are the bones.
2. The ligaments, called here sinews, are to be added in order to unite the bones, that the skeleton might be complete.
3. The flesh (the whole muscular system, the subjacent and superjacent muscles, including the arterial and venous system) clothes this skeleton.
4. The skin (the dermis and epidermis, or cutis and cuticle) envelopes the whole of these muscles or flesh; and now these bodies are in the state that the body of Adam was before it received the animal and intellectual principle from God.

---

[24] *The Wycliffe Bible Commentary*, Electronic Database. Copyright © 1962 by Moody Press.

5.   There was no breath in them – they had not yet received their souls.

6.   The wind, *ruwach* (OT: 7307), the soul, came into them. They were endued with animal and intellectual life; and they arose and evidenced a complete restoration to life, and began to perform its functions.'[25]

As well as there being many references to the importance of blood in the Scriptures, there are also some very interesting references to the importance of the bones. For example, notice that on the cross the soldiers did not break Jesus' legs:

> *'But when they came to Jesus and saw that He was already dead, they did not break His legs.'*
>
> (John 19:33)

The psalmist prophesies about Jesus that,

> *'He guards all his bones;*
> *Not one of them is broken.'*   (Psalm 34:20)

In the Old Testament, when the Jewish people were given directions regarding the time of the Passover, we read concerning the Passover lamb, in the book of Numbers,

> *'They shall leave none of it until morning, nor break one of its bones. According to all the ordinances of the Passover they shall keep it.'*   (Numbers 9:12)

---

[25] *Adam Clarke's Commentary*, Electronic Database. Copyright © 1996 by Biblesoft.

Jesus, the Passover lamb, was taken down from the cross before Shabbat. They could have realised that Jesus was already dead or conversely it could have been in fulfilment of the words concerning the Passover lamb,

> *'In one house it shall be eaten; you shall not carry any of the flesh outside the house, nor shall you break one of its bones.'* (Exodus 12:46)

How do we reconcile the two aspects: that 'life' seems to be both in the blood and in the bones? Could the answer lie in the **marrow** which is inside of the bones, for the marrow would seem to be related to both? Our blood is **made in the marrow** of the bones and some white cells are made in the spleen and the lymphatic system. About five million red cells are made every second in the bone marrow for our blood to stay healthy. The joints show that you are alive but it is the marrow that gives the life. It is worthy of note that in Hebrews 4:12 we are told that,

> *'the word of God is living and powerful, and sharper than any two-edged sword, piercing even to the division of soul and spirit, and of joints and marrow.'*

There was a very intriguing article in the *Times* newspaper (25th April 2004) entitled 'Hearts of dying patients repaired with injection of their own cells'. It concerns research into the transplant of stem cells for patients whose hearts were failing badly. Jonathan Leake, the science editor writes, 'The research patients were injected with stem cells taken from their own bone marrow. The cells – known for their power to grow into almost any type of human tissue –

quickly evolved into healthy heart cells that augmented and replaced their diseased predecessors. Robert Kormos, professor of surgery at the University of Pittsburgh School of Medicine, said it was the first convincing evidence that stem cell transplants could replace surgery as a way of treating heart failure.' Whilst it is important to note that this was very early research on a small (20) number of patients, nevertheless as Dr Amit Patel of Pittsburgh's McGowan Institute for Regenerative Medicine says, 'Stem cell transplantation led to significant improvement in cardiac function in these patients, compared with the 10 control patients who had just the bypass operations.'

It is very interesting to note that stem cells come from the bone marrow. We would suggest, therefore, that it is worth considering whether the blood, the marrow and the bones are all inter-related in answering the question: 'Where does "life" live?' If the premise is true there would be many repercussions for the healing ministry as to how we pray for others. For example, it may be that when we become bitter and envious of others in our spirit, this would have the potential of sending poisons into the blood stream. This poison may then begin to eat away at the bones. It is a well-known saying that what a person eats is not as important as what eats him! It would appear that to pray healing for the human spirit is as vital as to pray healing for the soul and for the body, for the 'life' flowing through the blood would depend upon the condition of the human spirit.

About the Author

Ruth was raised in the North East of England and trained as a primary school teacher taking her degree at Durham University. She has written and broadcast several children's stories on local radio and has a heart for hurting children (of whatever age) within the Body of Christ. She has two married daughters and several grandchildren. Along with her husband Joe, she has worked in the healing ministry for many years, both teaching and ministering into the lives of many hundreds of people. They were Directors of Ellel Ministries Centres in England and Canada for several years where they raised a number of prayer ministry teams. At present they are involved in training and establishing ministry teams in local church. Ruth is the author of a number of books on pastoral care: *Healing the Human Spirit, Healing Emotional Wounds, Freedom from Generational Sin, Praying for Children and Pastoral Prayer Ministry Teams in the Local Church.*

We hope you enjoyed reading this New Wine book.
For details of other New Wine books
and a wide range of titles from other
Word and Spirit publishers visit our website:
www.newwineministries.co.uk
email: newwine@xalt.co.uk